This is Volume 2 of three v
Artisans of Peace Overcoming Poverty

- Volume 1: A People-Centered Movement
- Volume 2: Defending Human Rights
- Volume 3: Understanding the Violence of Poverty

See page 145 for details about the contents of the other volumes.

Other publications by ATD Fourth World:

- *The Roles We Play: Recognising the Contribution of People in Poverty*, featuring photography by Eva Sajovic. (London, UK: 2014)

- *Challenge 2015: Towards Sustainable Development That Leaves No One Behind*, edited by Brendan Coyne, Xavier Godinot, Quyen Tran, and Thierry Viard. (Paris, France: 2014)

- *Not Meant to Live Like This: Weathering the Storm of Our Lives in New Orleans,* edited by M.G. Olsen, Karen Stornelli, and Maria Victoire, and with a foreword by William Julius Wilson. (Washington, DC: 2012)

- *Extreme Poverty Is Violence — Breaking the Silence — Searching for Peace,* by Anne-Claire Brand, Gérard Bureau, Martine Le Corre, Beatriz Monje Barón, and Rosalbina Pérez. (Vauréal, France: 2012)

- *Come With Us: Let's Make the World a Better Place,* a DVD by children from the Tapori Movement. (Geneva, Switzerland: 2009)

- *Unleashing Hidden Potential: How Parents, Teachers, Community Workers, and Academics Came Together to Improve Learning for Children in Poverty,* a CD-ROM by Carl Egner, Denis Cretinon, Jill Cunningham, Colette Jay, and Haruko Yamauchi. (Landover, MD: 2007)

- *How Poverty Separates Parents and Children: A Challenge to Human Rights,* edited by Diana Skelton and Valérie Brunner. (Méry-sur-Oise, France: 2004)

Artisans of Peace
Overcoming Poverty

VOLUME 2

Artisans of Peace Overcoming Poverty

VOLUME 2

Defending Human Rights

by Diana Faujour Skelton

with contributions from Anne-Sylvie Laurent
and Marie-Ange Libert

Published by ATD Fourth World: All Together in Dignity

Under the coordination of: Isabelle Pypaert Perrin, Jacqueline Plaisir, Diana Skelton, and Jean Toussaint

Cover design, interior design, and composition: Leigh McLellan Design

Coordination of photos: Jill Cunningham

Cover mosaic: Clotilde Chevalier of Coccinelle Graphisme Print and Cie

Photography: ATD Fourth World, Romain Fossey, and François Phliponeau

12 Rue Pasteur
95480 Pierrelaye
France
Telephone: 33-1-30-36-22-24
www.atd-fourthworld.org
E-mail: dg@atd-fourthworld.org

P.O. Box 1787
Gallup, New Mexico 87305
USA
Telephone: 1-301-832-1640

Date of publication: 2016, Pierrelaye, France

Printed by CreateSpace

ISBN-13: 978-1523851874

Cover photos in Manila, Philippines: Joy and her son, in front of their home under a bridge where they lived until the entire community was resettled outside the capital.

Contents

Introduction

Peace cannot be kept by force; it can only be achieved by understanding.

— Albert Einstein

When we live in poverty, we want to get back our rights, but we are not listened to. People have asked me why I haven't accused all of the people who have done my family so much wrong. I didn't testify in court because I thought that [those men] would kill me if I claimed my rights. I know that violence leads to more violence. [...But] there is always someone among us who appeals for peace so that we can live decently. That's how Merita was.

— Ivanite Saint-Clair, member of ATD Fourth World in Haiti

Day after day, families who are resisting the injustice and violence of extreme poverty find ways to strive toward peace. Merita Colot (whose story we told in Volume 1 of Artisans of Peace Overcoming Poverty) did this by taking risks in her community to create places where children could learn, and by reminding young people that she believed in their capacity to do better than to succumb to anger rooted in poverty and despair. The peace that Merita and others carry inside themselves enables them to inspire, to rebuild, to rethink their life choices, and to change their ways of being. It is a peace that opens people to possibilities of freedom.

In 1948, the United Nations adopted the Universal Declaration of Human Rights to express an ideal: that all people, in every country, could enjoy freedom from fear and freedom from want, and that "all human beings are born free and equal in dignity and rights." But expressing this ideal in a declaration was not enough for it to become a reality. People born into poverty continue to endure the denial of their rights.

Even during the decades following 1948, when movements began advancing on behalf of women's rights, of the civil rights of racial and ethnic minorities, and of people born into colonization, poverty was not yet seen as a human rights issue. Many people maintain that the rising tide of economic development will eventually lift all boats, and that everyone has the chance to work their way out of poverty. Some believe that poverty is a question of fate, and that it is impossible for all people to have a decent life. Still other people and institutions have become tangled in ideological power struggles about rights, losing sight of the fact that human dignity itself is denied by chronic poverty.

Given these challenges, it took many years for the United Nations to carry out human rights work on behalf of people in poverty — and its success is due to the contributions of people in poverty themselves. A human rights approach is not a policy handed down from above, but one based on the agency and free participation of all people. One of the landmark moments in the movement for the human rights of people in poverty took place in 1987 when Joseph Wresinski, the founder of ATD Fourth World, who was himself born into poverty, called on all members of society to come together to ensure that the human rights of people in poverty would actually be respected. On October 17, 1987, as noted in Volume 1, 100,000 people traveled from around the world to Paris, where Wresinski inaugurated a commemorative stone on the Plaza of Human Rights and Liberties. The words engraved there say:

Wherever men and women are condemned to live in extreme poverty,
human rights are violated.
To come together to ensure that these rights be respected
is our solemn duty.

Because of that message, which Wresinski also brought to the United Nations Commission on Human Rights, work began on the relationship between extreme poverty and human rights. This work, detailed in chapter 3 of this volume, was carried out together with people in poverty whose dignity has consistently been denied. It contributed to what in 2012 became the UN's Guiding Principles on Extreme Poverty and Human Rights. The Principles are the first worldwide policy guidelines to focus specifically on the human rights of people living in poverty. The Guiding Principles are unique because they draw directly on the experience and knowledge of people in poverty, and are rooted in their agency and empowerment.

The French term for poverty used most often by Wresinski, and engraved on the commemorative stone, was "la misère," a word harking back to Victor Hugo's *Les Misérables*. Often used by French-speaking people living in poverty to describe their own situation, this word is sometimes translated as "destitution" but lacks an identical expression in other languages, which is why the United Nations chose instead to use the term "extreme poverty." Unfortunately, this term is also often used by statisticians to categorize people and set them apart; whereas ATD Fourth World's aim is to strengthen solidarity among all people so that all poverty can one day be overcome. When we do use the term "extreme poverty," it is with the concern that many programs in low-income communities begin and end with the people who are the easiest to reach — people who are already well positioned to take advantage of development projects. Our experience has shown us that designing and evaluating programs together with the people who are the hardest to reach — people whose destitution has isolated them — can improve the lives of entire communities, leaving no one behind.

This volume is inspired by people living in poverty who are contributing to the world's understanding that there is no true peace without respect for the human rights of all people. In low-income communities around the world, people whose daily lives are hard have long been reaching out to one another in solidarity and standing up to injustice. Their efforts, too long unnoticed, are part of a small but growing movement that can help our whole society learn to develop a new culture where the rights and dignity of every person, family, and community will be respected.

1

Ensuring Protection and Support to Syrian Refugees in Lebanon

Previously strong economic growth rates in Lebanon have been negatively affected by political instability, security incidents, and the effects of the crisis in the Syrian Arab Republic. [...]According to current projections, there will be over 1.3 million registered Syrian refugees in Lebanon at the start of 2015.

— Office of the UN High Commissioner for Refugees[1]

Everyone is entitled to all the rights and freedoms set forth in this Declaration, without distinction of any kind, such as [...] national or social origin, property, birth, or other status. Furthermore, no distinction shall be made on the basis of the political, jurisdictional, or international status of the country or territory to which a person belongs.

— Universal Declaration of Human Rights

For Lebanon, a country with fewer than five million inhabitants, the rapid influx of more than a million refugees from Syria presents colossal challenges. Just what does it mean for everyone to be entitled to the right to live on this crowded planet, regardless of national origin? Whose lives are most powerfully impacted when refugees flood into a country? How does this change their lives? What choices do they make in the name of the right of all people to live in dignity?

Defending the human rights of all is a palpable daily challenge in low-income neighborhoods like Naba'a Bourj Hamoud, a densely populated and particularly diverse district on the edge of Beirut. While the Lebanese civil war increased sectarian segregation in many parts of the country, Naba'a remained home both to Muslims and to Christians. Since the war's end in 1990, buildings have remained pockmarked with

---

1. UNHCR Country Operations Profiles, 2013 and 2014.

Beirut, Lebanon: The neighborhood of Naba'a Bourj Hamoud.

bullet holes. Some elderly people in Naba'a have no relatives to care for them and live under bridges or beg to survive. The district's population has continued to grow, with foreign laborers, migrant workers, and asylum seekers arriving from Egypt, India, Iraq, Jordan, Nigeria, the Philippines, Sri Lanka, Sudan, Syria, and elsewhere.

Many residents of Naba'a have no identity papers. Some cannot obtain papers because their country of origin does not recognize their existence, including children born to parents of different religions in a country that forbids mixed marriage. Depending on their country of origin, they may also feel they are part of a group that others consider dangerous. There are also many women who arrive in Lebanon as domestic workers whose economic contribution to the country is not valued by others and whose employers often treat them badly or abuse them. If these women give birth to children in Lebanon, the children will have no identity papers unless their fathers recognize their paternity. Some of these people whose right to a legal identity is violated say, "No one wants me to exist."

As the Syrian civil war worsened in January 2013, one of ATD Fourth World's members in Naba'a wrote:

Naba'a is becoming more Syrian. Rents have increased so much that little by little people can't afford them and have to move out. The Syrians who arrive are crowding several families into single apartments to be able to afford the rent. Many are Kurdish families who are now our immediate neighbors. They are encouraging one another to come to Beitouna.

The leading Lebanese newspaper, *An-Nahar*, depicted the welcoming spirit of Beitouna in this 2012 article. The title reads, "Beitouna: the door is open to all."

Beitouna, "our house," is a small non-profit center where everyone is welcome, and where the shared priority is looking for ways to reach out to and support people in the most difficult situations. Since 2002 Beitouna has been closely linked to ATD Fourth World through our Forum on Overcoming Extreme Poverty.[2] Members of Beitouna say:

- "We teach our children to live together."
- "People meet here to be together and to be a source of strength for one another."
- "Being from the Sudan, we were rejected in other neighborhoods just because we're black. Here in Naba'a, I feel that we're accepted, and so we're safe."
- "Someone who comes to Beitouna has made a commitment."
- "Here, we learn that each of us matters — not because we're given anything material, but because there's a presence, a closeness to anyone who walks in."

---

2. This Forum, organized by ATD Fourth World, consists of a network of correspondence linking almost 3,500 people or organizations in 130 countries.

Families march through the Naba'a neighborhood to mark the World Day for
Overcoming Poverty: children hold high their ideas for a "Village of Peace," while
mothers from Beitouna carry posters showing words that give them courage.

For the 2013 World Day for Overcoming Poverty, on October 17,
the message written by members of Beitouna to others around the world
began by recalling what it means for the Lebanese people to see so many
Syrians arriving:

> *It's not easy for anyone. The two countries have had a difficult
> relationship, especially during the harsh Lebanese civil war. Many
> Lebanese still resent or distrust Syria. Here at Beitouna, we all feel
> a duty to be close to the Syrians because Lebanon has been through
> this: the anguish, the bereavement, being displaced, losing our homes.
> But there's also a challenge because everything can drive us to think,
> "Serves them right, it's their turn now." Some of us feel empathy for
> the suffering of the refugees, while others just can't. This is the context
> in which we are searching for what our relationships should be.*

Sayed Id, a father who is part of the Beitouna community, has experienced the mistrust that exists in Lebanon and speaks of how he overcame it:

> *Last month, I heard on the radio that a child in the hospital needed
> a blood donor. So I went to the hospital to give blood. But I was told,
> "Foreigners can't give blood here." I asked to meet the child's parents.
> The father told me to stay, and I was able to give blood after all. I am
> stronger because I participate in a group with others. Alone, I would*

do nothing. Here, I listen to others, we meet together to live out what we speak about. This gives real strength that you wouldn't always have alone.

The Story Garden: Children's right to "a place for co-existence, culture, and joy"

As more and more Syrian refugees streamed into the neighborhood, participants in Beitouna's Mothers' Group went out of their way to be welcoming, showing the Syrians where to find housing, food, clothing, and schools. This has led the newcomers to allow their children to participate in Beitouna's cultural activities. In its Story Garden, Beitouna's strongest priority is to create ways for children of different origins to mix, learn to cooperate, and make friends with one another. The women and teenagers who run this activity feel that it is particularly important for them to seek out and welcome the newest arrivals in the neighborhood by picking them up before the activity and taking them back afterwards to their new homes. While the activities used to involve about twenty children, in 2014 they grew to involve a hundred.

Children view a photographic timeline showing their families' involvement in Beitouna's fifteen-year history.

October 2013: on the World Day for Overcoming Poverty, starting off
a march from the Naba'a neighborhood to a nearby public garden.

Elie D.[3] is one of the teenagers who sometimes help mothers to run
the Story Garden. Years ago, his family came from Syria to Lebanon,
where they had nowhere to live and had to sleep in a car. In 2010, although
Elie's family members continued to face enormous challenges in their
own daily lives, Elie, then 11, was so shocked by news of the devastation
of the earthquake in Haiti that he initiated a campaign to send support to
Haiti. In a cybercafé, he downloaded photos of the destruction to show his
neighbors. Speaking to a group of sixty people, he asked them to imagine
themselves as the children in Port-au-Prince playing on the ground when
it started to tremble beneath them. Inspired by his concern, many people
in Naba'a wrote messages of support or made donations for the people of
Haiti. Today, he and other teenagers feel responsible for the younger children at Beitouna. In the summer of 2013, when the adults running the
Story Garden saw that the increased numbers of children led to difficulties
among some of them, Elie and two other teenagers — Bakair and Yvonne
— separated the Story Garden participants into smaller groups by age so
they could make sure that no child felt left out, and that everyone would
be able to participate fully and complete the activities. For these teenagers

3. Teenagers are referred to by first name only.

and others, Beitouna has been a place where they learn to live peacefully in a diverse community. Jamil, for example, has come to know Elie M. through the Beitouna youth group. Despite their different religions and the religious conflict in their country's past, Jamil says today, "Elie is like my brother. We'll always be there for each other, no matter what."

In addition to rent increases, there have been many challenges caused by the influx of new people, both in the neighborhood and at Beitouna's small center, which is located in two rooms on the ground floor of a run-down apartment building. These rooms house Beitouna's meetings for parents and its cooperative grocery system. Some of the newcomers from Syria have begun to help organize these activities. Other residents in the building — some of whom have relatives who were killed recently in armed conflict — have complained to Beitouna staff about so many people coming in and out. The members of Beitouna feel that their center is too small now. Participants in the Mothers' Group, who all volunteer their time despite their own difficult lives, sometimes feel overwhelmed by need. They can feel that their own families are losing out as the country's resources are stretched ever thinner. Sometimes they disagree about how to choose priorities when lack of time, space, or other resources limits their activities. They also see that the refugees "…are afraid of one another," as one mother wrote. "They need a community, but at the same time they don't trust others."

Abir Rizk, a Syrian mother, has been involved with Beitouna for several years. Because of her close links with her neighbors in Naba'a, as well as with the refugees arriving from Syria, she has witnessed some very concrete difficulties:

> In the neighborhood, we often set off firecrackers; it's the Lebanese way to celebrate. But Syrian children are terrified of the firecrackers. [...] Yesterday, in front of our building, there was a car for a wedding, a very beautiful car. My upstairs neighbors, who are Syrian, suddenly dumped dirty water onto the car. The bridal couple got angry at me, because they know me, and because I'm Syrian too. So I went to talk to my neighbors. They asked, "How can others be celebrating when people in our country are dying every day?" Luckily, these neighbors did apologize to the bridal couple, but this incident could have caused a big problem in our neighborhood. For my part,

For the World Day for Overcoming Poverty, children paraded through the Naba'a neighborhood with posters for their "Village of Peace."

I'm often torn: Peace or anger? Spite or concern for others? I've lived with anguish, but also with fulfillment.

Despite these difficulties, Beitouna's Mothers' Group chooses to continue offering support because:

At Beitouna, we learn the value of being open. As mothers, it is our responsibility to teach this to our children. We help one another because we want to bring the children out of war and to give them joy. The Story Garden brings all our children together. It's a place for co-existence, for culture, and for joy shared by all of us. Opening our hearts is the most important thing. What matters is a personal relationship of friendship, and thinking of each person's dignity. Whether we are Lebanese or foreigners, we have the same need to feel solidarity and to give one another strength. When we encourage the refugees, we can see that they are touched and that they feel safe here. Even with children who beg in the streets, little by little, we are able to be closer. We've tried to respond to everyone who comes to our door. But many do not come to our door and must be in even more difficult situations. We only wish we had the means to do more.

Although Mrs. Rizk sometimes feels torn between peace and anger, she concludes: "In fact, it's this neighborhood that has given me strength. When I first arrived, my children were young. I was from somewhere else. I was concerned about whether my little family would be all right

Children from
Beitouna show
some essentials
for their "Village
of Peace."

here and whether the place was safe. It wasn't the life I'd dreamed of. But I said to myself, 'My life is here now, this is where I'll live it.' And I began to love this neighborhood with everything about it."

On the World Day for Overcoming Poverty: "No walls between us"

Mohammad El Omar, one of the Syrian refugees who arrived recently in Naba'a says, "Beitouna is small, but what you've done here is very big. It matters so much that you've built a close-knit community linking people who are so different, with no walls between us. This is the basis for being able to take new steps forward. We have a solid foundation." One such step forward was taken by dozens of families on the World Day for Overcoming Poverty in 2013. They sang as they marched from Beitouna to a public garden in the Sin El Fil neighborhood, where they held a commemoration. To prepare for the march, children painted posters showing everything they dream of having in a Village of Peace: schools, homes, friendship, flowers — and as many colors as possible. Mothers made their own posters, using calligraphy to write the words that give them strength to fight poverty every day: togetherness, faith, peace, family, solidarity, dignity, sincerity, love, patience, generosity, sacrifice, and persistence.

During the commemoration, fathers acted out a skit, telling the story of how they were able to help an elderly Palestinian man as he was dying, and to ensure that he received a decent burial. They called for solidarity to reach all those who are struggling, from Palestine, Syria, and elsewhere.

For October 17, World Day for Overcoming Poverty, fathers from Beitouna perform a skit to show that solidarity must be extended to all.

The events of the day included exchanging messages of encouragement with members of ATD Fourth World in the Central African Republic, Egypt, France, and Senegal. In Beitouna's message, members spoke about the camping trip that Beitouna organizes every summer. These group trips enable Christian and Muslim families alike, and in particular those whose lives are hard, to get out of the city together, to enjoy staying in tents in the woods and sharing open-air meals. Dozens of families have participated. The best part, the families say, is being able, for a short time, to be free from the anxiety of making ends meet. In their message[4] for the World Day, they wrote:

Pami and her husband came to Lebanon from India. He had a job and they had two children. But when their youngest was only one year old, the father died suddenly. Pami spoke very little Arabic and didn't know where to go. She had always counted on her husband in this country she doesn't know well. Actually, we Lebanese scare her a little bit. So we began helping her with daily life, and we invited her family to our summer camp. Pami thought it would be stressful to live with other families every day, so she made excuses to say no: "My son has no shoes." Or, "I can't eat beef, it's against my religion." Of course we could easily solve these questions. Barbara, who has six children, encouraged Pami, telling her that Barbara's sons like playing with Pami's. Finally, she came and was happy for the whole

4. http://refuserlamisere.org/temoignages/lb/any-tag

Sr. Thérèse Ricard, center,
at a 2014 celebration of
Beitouna's fifteen-year
history.

*time. And when we returned to Naba'a, she had made new friends.
She's no longer scared, and stops in to chat with others. She built
links for her future.*

*When we are overcoming poverty, who is on the front lines? Do
we know their names? They are not people in the news, not champion
athletes, or Nobel prize winners, or saints! No, the people on the front
lines are the ones who aren't usually seen, the poorest of every society.
Today, we remember and honor them. We recognize the value of
their lives. We are thinking with sorrow of those who died trying*

A testament to Beitouna's diversity and richness: committee
members of Egyptian, Kurdish, Sri-Lankan, and Sudanese origins.

to escape poverty, like those from Akkar.[5] We will now plant a tree to
bear witness to our convictions, our efforts, and our commitment.

• • •

Beitouna has been present in Naba'a since 1999. To mark its 15th anni-
versary, all its members reflected on the past to learn from their history
together. Sr. Thérèse Ricard, who has played a central role in Beitouna
since 2000, said:

> *Often we think of the history of wars, of politicians and public
> figures, but not of the ordinary people who experienced history.
> These ordinary children and families gave us the soil in which our
> own lives took root, even if we don't know their names. This is
> history: each person matters for those who follow.*

This conviction that each person matters is at the heart of Beitouna's
efforts to defend the right for everyone to be able to live in dignity. In the
public hallway of the dilapidated apartment building where Beitouna's
members meet, Joseph Wresinski's words are posted:

> *Wherever men and women are condemned to live in extreme poverty,
> human rights are violated.
> To come together to ensure that these rights be respected
> is our solemn duty.*

Whether it is poverty or armed conflict that threatens a person's human rights, the weight of responsibility underlying these words is evident
to the residents of Naba'a. Their housing, schools, and other community
resources have been stretched thin by the unending arrival of refugees.
Despite this, they have chosen together to shoulder the weight of this
responsibility, determined to welcome diversity and to ensure that no
one's rights be denied.

---

5. Dozens of Lebanese from Akkar drowned trying to reach Australia. "Asylum-Seekers
Drown Off Indonesia Coast," *Al-Jazeera*, September 28, 2013.

2

A New Start:
Mass Resettlement in the Philippines

This chapter describes our work in the Philippines with some of the most fragile families who live in poverty, and in particular how they experience government efforts to help them in a series of mass resettlements. In the letter below, Anne-Sylvie Laurent of ATD Fourth World's team in Manila writes about one of these resettlements:

August 28, 2014 — *Today marks a step forward for the families still living under the bridge in the Tulay community. About half of them are leaving, their homes demolished and with no possibility of returning. In the span of one night, these homes disappeared. The people here — especially the ones being relocated today — did not have a minute of sleep last night. They were busy packing, and then dismantling their homes, a requirement for being resettled. One of*

Until 2014, about a hundred families, like that of Ms. Josephine, above, made their homes suspended from the underside of a bridge in the Tulay community of Manila.

the mothers says she can't relocate today, but her home is almost completely gone, only the floor remaining. Everything looks very different with so many homes gone, leaving only bare framework supporting other homes.

They were told yesterday to have their belongings ready at 6 a.m., but the moving trucks have not yet come. At 9 a.m., two trucks arrive, but their doors remain closed. People are exhausted and miserable, especially when it starts to drizzle. Then the rain begins to pour and everyone's belongings get soaked. It is obvious that not all of the belongings would fit in two trucks, but no other vehicle arrives. Because of the limited space, people will not be allowed to transport the wood from the homes they demolished. Some of the young men are already scavenging in the estuary below for fallen pieces of wood they can sell. […] Finally, an announcement is made by loudspeaker, telling everyone to line up so their blood pressure can be checked before the departure.

One mother says she saw one of the movers from the truck take a clean shirt out of her packed bag, use it to wipe his face and arms, and then throw it away. She has heard that some people's personal property was stolen when they arrived at the resettlement site, and she is worried that today she or others will lose some of their few, precious belongings. […]

When we arrive at the site, it is 4 p.m. Each person is given a ticket with a block and lot number. One of the women stands alone, without her family. She cannot read the ticket, so together we look for her new home. […] There are weeds everywhere up to our knees, but soon many families are busy removing them, sharing tools, and helping each other. Banishing the weeds quickly is a question of self-respect.

This resettlement is a colossal human and logistical challenge. The Filipino government has counted a hundred thousand households in dangerous informal settlements in the Metro Manila area, sixty thousand of them less than three meters from a waterway. On the underside of the Tulay bridge in the heart of Manila, homes are suspended right above the water. Rising sea levels are exacerbating the effects of the regular typhoons and floods that have long endangered the inhabitants' lives.

2014: Homes under the bridge of the Tulay community being dismantled.

As global warming worsens flooding in many parts of the world, more mass resettlements will be needed. ThinkProgress reports, "Climate change is making even 'normal' weather patterns more disaster-prone. [...] There is no question that extreme weather events are on the rise in the South Pacific [...] and the Philippines is one of the top five most affected countries."[6] Our team's long history in the Tulay community there has put us in a key position to focus on the most fragile families while also continuing to learn from the stronger families and fostering mutual support throughout the community. Despite our team's involvement, the most fragile families have been doing much worse than the others, and more support is clearly needed.

ATD Fourth World has been present in the Tulay community under the bridge since 1989. We run cultural and educational activities with the children and organize Community Forums where adults from different parts of Manila meet to express their ideas and participate in community

---

6. Page, Samantha. "Philippines Braces For Climate Change, and the Aid Community Adapts," *ThinkProgress*, March 20, 2015.

Residents under the bridge in Tulay often earned a living by selling food or other small items to people in vehicles passing over the bridge.

(Below) Families in the Tulay community in Manila built their homes using only scrap wood and ingenuity.

life. The homes under this bridge were cramped and crowded, shaken with every truck that rolled across the bridge. Residents were continually exposed to water-borne disease. And yet, living in such a busy urban area, the residents were usually able to earn money by selling food or small, practical items to drivers stuck in traffic jams. Because they could make a living here, about a hundred families built their homes on the underside of the bridge, using only scrap wood and ingenuity. Resettling now in completely new and less populated areas, many people with limited formal education and job skills must immediately find completely new ways to earn money. Nevertheless, the National Housing Authority's offer — one room per family in a block of low buildings with a thirty-year mortgage — leads community members to dream that this once-in-a-lifetime chance is a "gift of God" that some have said "could be my legacy to my children."

Failed resettlements in the past

Resettlements like this one have been taking place since 1987 in Metro Manila, where one community where we know residents was part of a mass resettlement project in 2005. The pace of resettlements increased in 2008 when the Filipino Supreme Court ordered the government to clean Manila's waterways of the pollution that is inevitably worsened by overcrowding and lack of wastewater treatment plants. In 2012, the Department of the Interior and Local Government (DILG) targeted twenty thousand families to be relocated the following year,[7] saying that it "intends to relocate two hundred informal settler families every week."[8]

In the past, many people left their informal homes in Manila to be resettled about twenty-five miles away. Some of these families managed to remain there despite the difficulties. One family who used to live under the Tulay bridge was resettled in Cabuyao, about thirty miles south of Manila. On a visit back to Tulay after ten years away, their 11-year-old

7. Ranada, Pia. "Year-end target: Relocation of 20,000 Manila families," Rappler social news network, October 25, 2013.

8. "Government to Relocate More Informal Settlers from Metro Manila Danger Zones," DILG website, July 25, 2014.

child was struck by the contrasts and said, "Imagine: before, our family too was begging at the stoplight."[9]

Others, however, found no way to earn money near the resettlement sites. Worse, life was much more expensive in their new homes. Along the waterways, rent was either free or very cheap; water was free and nearby, though polluted; and people bought electricity only when they could afford it. These are characteristics of many informal settlements where people are forced to live because they cannot afford rent and utilities elsewhere. In the new homes, people had to buy water at a pump, truck, or reservoir, and carry it a long way home. There were fees for garbage pick-up. Electricity remained on all the time and the bills had to be paid regularly. Mortgage payments began a year after a family moved in. If work could not be found, there was no choice but to send a breadwinner back to Manila to continue earning money in familiar ways. Because these trips were long and expensive, breadwinners often returned to live in Manila, visiting their families only on some weekends when they could afford it. Clearly this wasn't an option for single-parent families, who often found life impossible in the new housing sites.

Some families gave up their new homes to return to Manila for good. According to the Rappler social news network, in 2005, one family was relocated to Laguna, seventy miles southeast of Manila, "only to return under the bridge after a year due to a lack of job opportunities and of access to basic social services. The mother lamented, 'Hospitals are really far away [from the resettlement site]; sometimes they charge, too. If you have an emergency, you need to pay a hefty price' for pedicab fare to get to the hospital."[10] Another mother recalled:

> *For ten years, my family lived in a relocation site in Bulacan [seven miles north of Manila], while my husband worked in Manila. Then he was without work for more than a year, and we had almost nothing to eat. Most of the people around us were poor, too; it was difficult to*

---

9. Although this chapter quotes several people living in poverty, and was written in consultation with some of them, most chose not to be named here in order to protect their privacy.

10. Gavilan, Jodesz. "Families living under Quirino Bridge strive to survive," Rappler, June 4, 2014.

A new resettlement site in Norzagaray. Although new residents arrive regularly here and in other sites, some leave because they are unable to earn a living. This can result in entire rows of uninhabited homes.

find families who could pay us to wash clothes or do other jobs. That's why we came back to live in our former place under a bridge.

The government resettled families in a number of ways, such as offering the one-year deferment of mortgage payments. Some received lump-sum subsidies so that they could build their own home. However, families who accepted this support but eventually moved back to Manila are not eligible to be rehoused a second time. Having left the city with high hopes, families who were driven to return were deeply disappointed by this situation.

Officials, too, are frustrated by these returns. Occasionally, one will express this in insults, saying, "You know, there's a name for families like you: professional squatters." The term "professional squatter" is in fact the only way that returnees are described in the Urban Development and Housing Act. The only possibility for returnees to be relocated again is if they have children over 18 who are starting their own families, in which case the adult children can apply to be resettled together with their parents. Some administrators say, "The young people in these families who came back got married and had a child just in order to benefit from relocation." This frustration is sometimes generalized to include the entire Tulay community, although most of the families were never relocated before. One administrator said, "We need to put all the resettlements here on hold to weed out the returnees." However, in this community, none of the returnees dared to reapply.

There is also a cut-off age for the resettlement, with some people too old to be included. The exact age is not clearly stated and some people have been given conflicting information as to whether or not they meet the age criterion. A couple aged 58 and 59 were told that because of their age they would need to submit a waiver and find a younger applicant to live with, but when they tried to apply with the husband's younger brother, they were refused and told to apply with their son's already crowded family.

Some people who still remain under the bridge are trying to finish the paperwork to qualify for resettlement. Others did not manage to apply in time. One couple delayed the relocation of their daughter because at the time they were resettled, the daughter was in the running to become valedictorian and did not want to change schools. The daughter stayed behind, together with her grandparents, who said, "If needed we would be happy to sleep on the sidewalk, but we do not want this for her. We prefer for her to sleep under the bridge because it is safer." (In March 2015, the

After Cienna's home under the bridge was demolished, she stayed in Manila to continue her schooling. In March 2015, she was named her school's valedictorian. Here, she leads the singing during a 2014 ATD Festival of Learning in Tulay.

girl, Cienna Charisse Igano, did in fact become her elementary school's valedictorian, while still sleeping under the bridge.[11]) As the community empties, with more and more families leaving and homes being demolished, the only certainty is that no one will be allowed to remain along the waterways and that any new returnees will be forbidden to live there. It is not clear where people who are not eligible for resettlement will live.

The role of ATD Fourth World's team

ATD Fourth World's cultural activities in Manila have long included families in two informal settlements: under the Tulay bridge and in the North Cemetery. In a third settlement, on a loading dock in Navotas (on the northwest coast of Manila), work has been carried out in partnership with the Sisters of the Good News–Fourth World. Within each of these communities, some families are stronger and more dynamic, while others are much more fragile. When the resettlement process began, our team feared that the most vulnerable families would not be able to benefit without extra support.

In fact, this is what is happening with the Manila resettlement project. The scale of the project and the number of implementing agencies prevent the authorities from taking into account the very different levels of poverty in the informal settlements. Our team decided that, in addition to our projects with children and adults, it would also make a point of offering intensive support to the most vulnerable families throughout the resettlement process. At the same time, we continued to stay in touch with more dynamic families in order to learn from their strategies, support solidarity among all the families, and compare the experiences of both groups.

To offer this intensive support, our team, in consultation with young community members who help us facilitate literacy activities, first identified twenty-five priority families who we believed might have trouble with the resettlement process. These are families for whom life is a constant series of emergencies. The parents have a low level of literacy and the children are behind in school or not enrolled at all. They lack identity

---

11. "Class Valedictorian from Paco Lives Under a Bridge," *GMA News Online*, March 18, 2015.

Community knowledge: Diana and Cathy, young community members, help support families' aspirations for their children by facilitating Street Libraries and Festivals of Learning.

Storytime during a Street Library in Tulay. Street Libraries cultivate a love of books and culture throughout the entire community.

papers, or their official documents contain errors. They do not have connections with other non-profit groups. Their extended families are unable to support them in times of difficulty. They may be criticized by others in their community. They are vulnerable to gang violence and to police abuse. They may get in trouble with district watchmen for being caught begging. Some of them are returnees and will receive no further government support.

Families who have lived along certain waterways that must be cleaned may receive up to $400[12] from the government, intended to help them find a way to earn money in the resettlement areas. However, families being resettled from other waterways may receive no cash at all, or only one day's worth of groceries to help them move out of the city.[13] While stronger families who receive the subsidy may take advantage of it to succeed, even this opportunity for investment is not enough for the priority families, particularly in the highly competitive atmosphere where everyone is trying to establish a livelihood. The priority families more often have debts to repay and unexpected crises that make it impossible for them to save money, even if their activity is profitable. They may have the best intentions, but they cannot hold onto money for long.

Our current projects for children are Street Libraries, which incorporate stories and creative activities outdoors in view of the community, and a literacy program called "Ang Galing!" (meaning "Awesome!"). The literacy program offers a positive learning experience for children who struggle academically or are not attending school. The Street Libraries and an annual Festival of Learning promote a love of books and culture for a wider range of children. All these projects now take place from two to four times a month in five communities: under the Tulay bridge for as long as children remain there; in an informal settlement in Manila North Cemetery where thousands of families live and work to maintain the mausoleums; and in three of the sites (Calauan, Norzagaray, and Pandi) where families from Tulay have been resettled.

We continue to organize Community Forums that gather people from several communities to talk about their experiences, express their thoughts, and dialogue with guest speakers. In addition, wherever priority families have been relocated (Balagtas, Calauan, Norzagaray, and Pandi), we run "Community Mini-Forums" either monthly or every other month. Our team prepares these through individual visits to different

---

12. All monetary amounts have been converted from Philippine pesos to U.S. dollars.
13. Gavilan, Jodesz. "Families living under Quirino Bridge strive to survive," *Rappler*, June 4, 2014.

The Ang Galing literacy program gives priority
to struggling students for personalized tutoring.

families. In addition to issues that were addressed in the past, such as
experiences with education or health care services, the Community Forums now also include discussions about the events linked to relocation
and about training to cope with new situations: budgeting, savings, financial literacy, family relationships, ways of making a living, and getting
to know the areas surrounding the resettlement sites. The Community
Forums have helped priority families to voice their concerns in dialogue
and correspondence with the agencies implementing the resettlement.

In addition, we continued to develop relationships between community members, agencies, and non-profit partners for a participatory
action-research project on housing and education.[14] This work, where
priority families and practitioners engaged in constructive dialogue about
social policy, shows that a similar approach should be possible when planning resettlements.

---

14. The findings of this project, run by UNICEF and ATD Fourth World–Philippines,
are reported in "Partners in development: Listening to the voices of families living in
extreme poverty. A contribution to the post-2015 Sustainable Development Agenda,"
2015. http://bit.ly/ATD-PH-PartnersInDevelopment

Preparing for resettlement

Beginning in 2013, we helped community members to develop relationships with the different implementing agencies and have a voice in the resettlement process. During 2014 our team made more than twenty trips to visit four resettlement sites. For each site, one of these visits included a delegation of about ten community members who had not yet been resettled. On returning home, the delegates would share news with others who were going to be resettled. This prepared everyone to cope with the process, to study the challenges and opportunities of each site, and to judge the length of the commute likely to separate family members after the move. Several site visits were also organized by the implementing agencies; however, making an official site visit did not ensure that a person would be allowed to relocate to that site, which led to confusion and disappointment.

During these visits, community members were often glad to see housing made of concrete but worried about the sites' isolation and distance from Manila. Some are much farther away than previous resettlement sites, to which transportation costs about $5.40 for a round trip. The trip

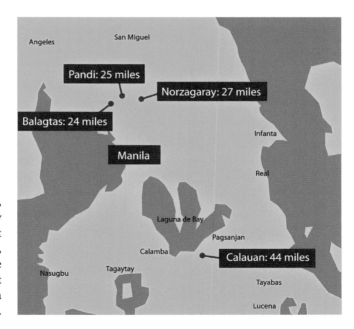

This map, drawn by artist Robert Alejandro, shows the resettlement sites in relation to Manila.

to Calauan from the city is so long and expensive that some parents who return to the city to work cannot visit their families more than once or twice a month. Pandi is closer and less expensive — about 25 miles and $3.85 — but the commute involves five forms of transportation: two jeeps, then a bus, then a pedicab, then another jeep. Because jeeps wait to fill up with passengers before leaving, the entire trip to Pandi can take as long as three hours. In weighing their options, community members' main concern was how to survive in these sites. Some opted for Calauan — the farthest — because they saw that there were several established non-profit organizations that could offer them support there. Others preferred the shortest possible distance from Manila, because they planned to return to the city to earn their livelihood.

In 2010, a Peace Corps volunteer described a first visit to one of the sites:

> *Guards waved our van inside the large gates. Several miles wide, the area once was a flat, grassy canvas of land sheltered only by the mountain behind it. Outside our window, at least a hundred rows of concrete housing are erected along the sparse green land. There are makeshift streets between the rows of housing. Each family lives in a single room of the open-windowed shelters. The buildings look much like bomb shelters, mere concrete shells. [...] Several men ride their pedicabs through the streets, selling crackers, cigarettes, and soda, though no buyers approach.*[15]

Three years later, a journalist reported on the Calauan site, giving a description that could also apply to any of the other sites visited by ATD Fourth World: "Many storms have passed and about nine hundred houses are either abandoned or remain unoccupied. Rows upon rows of row-houses are uninhabited. It's that part of town that is every square meter a ghost town. It's how life looks without people. Despite being given a place to live, the settlers have no place to make a living. [...] Without any livelihood, they are unable to pay the monthly [mortgage]. Although the houses have been ready for occupancy, they remain empty. [...] Some

---

15. The Peace Corps–Philippines. "Resettlement Project," "Pioneers! O Pioneers!" *Blog*, July 21, 2010.

Calauan resettlement site, September 2014: ATD volunteers bring
books and literacy games on visits, while some adults set up
small gardens among dozens of empty row houses.

heads of households leave to work in the city on weekdays, turning Bayan
ni Juan into a town without husbands and fathers. It has its own set of
complications and social implications."[16]

---

16. Moya, George P. "Failed relocation in 'Bayan ni Juan,'" *Rappler*, November 23, 2013.

When Tulay community members traveled with our team to visit people they knew who had been rehoused already, the news they heard was sometimes worrisome:

"I miss my wife and children; I can't afford to visit them more than once a month."

"During the week, when there are just a few people here, it is sad. I don't know what to do."

"My daughter misses her old teacher; she's afraid of the one here and doesn't go to school anymore."

"Water is too far away for us to fetch; we must pay someone who can carry it."

"Food here costs so much more than in Tulay!"

"If you come too, there will be more of us here going hungry! You have to adjust to hunger; at the beginning your stomach brings you pain."

Despite these reports, families still living in Tulay knew they, too, would have to leave their homes because, in addition to the waterway-cleaning plans, a superhighway is scheduled to pass through Tulay. As the resettlements progressed and residents saw their former neighbors' lodgings being demolished, it drove home to them that time was running out.

The most urgent need in early 2014 was to support priority families in obtaining the administrative papers needed for resettlement. At the beginning, information was unclear about what would be required of each family member and how a person whose birth was unregistered could apply. Rumors circulated that the family photo needed to show any relative who might want to visit.

In fact, copies of either birth registration or certification of no birth record are required from every family member. In addition, every head of household needs an application form, a police clearance, a valid ID, a local district certificate, an affidavit of income, a marriage certificate or affidavit of cohabitation, an individual ID photo, a family photograph, and a "house tagging number" proving the tenancy of a family in a zone slated for resettlement. Also if any family member is incarcerated at the time of the resettlement, a certificate of detention is required before the others can move.

A boy forgoes Street Library activities to collect water
for neighbors at the Calauan relocation site.

Our team decided to help as many people as possible to apply for copies of their birth registration or certification of no birth record. Although this certification can cost as much as $4.00 — a major expense for families barely scraping by — lacking one can result in being excluded in many situations. Often the people who fell the farthest behind in obtaining the required documents were those uncomfortable with reading and writing. Some need to sign documents with a thumbprint. When accompanying several priority families to an office to request birth certificates, Anne-Sylvie observed:

One mother's handwriting is fragile and can lead to mistakes — mistakes we don't want to have happen, as the spelling is of the utmost importance. The slightest error can mean that an existing registration will not be found, or that it will become necessary to provide an affidavit of discrepancy. Accompanying her means finding the right balance, allowing her to fill in her own application herself, but respectfully checking to correct the errors she has made. Another mother did not know her own date of birth.

A survey conducted in Tulay by our team found that out of 137 people, 35 either had no birth registration or had an error in their birth registration. Thus 26 percent of them lacked correct legal identity papers. In a few instances, public officials had made some of these errors, such as providing an ID from a national cash transfer program with a spelling mistake in a woman's name.

Choices taken away

For every family being resettled, navigating the process presented a challenge. In addition to confusing bureaucratic requirements, deadlines to be eligible for resettlement in specific sites were also unclear and often changed. These challenges made things particularly difficult for the families we consider our priority.

In February 2014, community members who had visited sites in Calauan and Balagtas had long debates about their comparative merits. Although Calauan is much farther from Manila, the cost of the mortgages in Balagtas was understood to be higher. Those resettled in Balagtas must pay mortgages for both their home and the land it is on, while those in one of the Calauan sites pay only for the lot, not the housing. Sometimes the projected date of a resettlement influenced people's choices. One mother, planning to travel to Saudi Arabia to work as a domestic, wanted to choose whichever site would be available first so that she could help her husband to move before leaving. Neighbors hoped to remain with the same neighbors by being resettled together; but in some cases even a wife and husband disagreed about which site would be better for them. No one wanted to be the only family from Tulay in a new site, especially given that couples were likely to be forced to live apart so that a breadwinner could earn money in Manila.

In fact, it soon became clear that Balagtas was considered full and no longer a possible choice. Nor did everyone want to go to Calauan. Several more sites where they might be sent instead were named shortly afterward. This caused anxiety. Discussing the short time left before the move, two mothers agreed, "I am not ready inside myself to move." Anne-Sylvie described daily life in Tulay: "People are constantly shaken. In the past, it was the heavy trucks passing over the bridge that shook their dwellings. Now it is the constantly changing news and all the uncertainty about

Community members try to stay informed despite the conflicting information often given by agencies.

the approaching relocation that are shaking their lives and making them feel deceived."

Throughout the process, it was difficult for community members and our team to stay informed. The resettlements have involved many agencies, and they often gave conflicting information. Some agencies are private non-profits; five are national government departments; others are local government units, both in Manila and in every resettlement site.

Our team supported priority families extensively in their efforts to communicate: typing emails dictated by adults who lacked the literacy skills to write directly; offering use of our cellphones and email address; accompanying people to various offices when they went to submit documents; and helping groups of adults to write collective letters. Anne-Sylvie noted, "Even when the administrators try their best to be approachable, they represent hierarchy and authority for some people who are shy about approaching them." Despite all this support, community members were often disappointed or frustrated because agencies regularly changed dates and possible relocation sites. The changes often caused families to miss deadlines if an agency to which they had submitted all their documents delayed in passing their files to other agencies. Some families had to pay for new documents when an agency lost the original ones they had submitted.

There was also confusion when community members saw empty homes on a site visit but were told that the site was full, with the remaining homes reserved for families from other places. For example, twelve families from Tulay were on a list for resettlement in Balagtas on April 29, 2014. Their move was rescheduled for May 29. At the last minute, after the families had washed and dried their laundry to pack everything, the resettlement was rescheduled again. Dictating to Anne-Sylvie, they wrote a letter to the local implementing agency, asking:

> *Why did the system change, with no more slots for us? We know that we pre-qualified. Our companions who relocated on April 22 tell us that there are still vacant houses. Ma'am, please, we really want to be relocated in Balagtas, because it is the closest to Manila, where we still have our livelihood. Also, some of us have family members already relocated in Balagtas and we wish to be together. We will pay for the house given to us. Surely, Ma'am, we are entitled to live in the area where we can best live.*

When community members visited the office to ask for a response to their letter, the explanation given was that there was no coordinating agency in charge of counting the available slots, so being endorsed did not guarantee a place, and there were no more slots in Balagtas. However, in Balagtas, at that time, some homes remained vacant, although deteriorated, and others were still being constructed. It seemed that these homes were reserved for families in informal settlements surrounding Balagtas. People from Manila would have to be resettled farther afield.

Rescheduling of resettlement dates had additional consequences. For instance, one family did not enroll its children in school at all for their last year in Tulay, thinking it would be better for them to begin after the resettlement, which was repeatedly delayed. Another mother took a leave of absence from her job in a hospital in order to move and then extended it so that she could go to appointments to have her documents verified when the resettlement was rescheduled. During her absence from work, she was replaced, and after that she was given only occasional shifts.

Sometimes an implementing agency would say, "People know they should have prepared their papers in advance, so if they haven't done it

Resettled families in Balagtas, connecting with residents in other relocation sites, display their part of the 2014 World Day for Overcoming Poverty slogan: "Think, Act, Decide Together with People in Extreme Poverty to Leave No One Behind."

yet, they are just not interested." In fact some people who were interested in moving chose to wait because they saw cases where delays in the resettlement process obliged their neighbors to pay a second time to obtain recent documents when the original ones were more than six months old. Because the dates for resettlement, first scheduled for early 2013, were repeatedly rescheduled throughout 2013 and 2014, it was hard for people to know whether it was better to prepare in advance or to wait and avoid paying twice. To compound the anxiety, the deadlines they were given for resettling were often very short. The community might be told on a Sunday night that a resettlement would take place the following Tuesday morning. Our team observed that when community members fell behind in obtaining their administrative papers, "it was not from lack of interest, but a more complex set of factors: lack of money, lack of confidence, and unfamiliarity with administration." For most community members, two years went by between the time they were notified to prepare their papers and their actual resettlement.

All these factors made it difficult to keep families together. Neighbors and extended families had hoped to be resettled on the same site to offer one another mutual support in new surroundings where most families must live far apart from a breadwinner who remains in the city. Now, however, they find themselves scattered across five different sites. Families who were not able to move on a specific day often had no choice but to change sites. One woman whose entire folder was lost by an implementing agency was not allowed to move on the same day as her sister's family. She was required to resubmit everything, and by the time that was done she was not allowed to move to the same site. For more than a year, the four households in her extended family had all been on the list for Calauan, but in the end only one household was allowed to move there. The others are now on the opposite side of Manila, about 70 miles north at two different sites in Pandi, which are not in walking distance of each other. Even for families in sites that are in the same province, visiting one another can require an expensive trip of two hours, via four modes of transportation.

In another family, a woman hoped to wait for her husband's release from prison before resettling so they could have a fresh start together. Anne-Sylvie noted, "Realizing that they too could soon have a house, I saw her relax, for just a fraction of a second. But her situation is difficult. In jail, her husband has contracted a lot of debt for medicine because he was ill. Her work is hard, collecting plastic bottles on the highway. Her worries still seem far too powerful for her to dare get her hopes up." The husband's release date was later postponed, and the family was not allowed to wait before relocating two and a half hours away. The son asked Anne-Sylvie, "When my dad gets out, will you show him how to find us now?"

Despite the complexity of the administrative process, some agency staff were particularly kind and helpful. The many administrators we met have been working very hard to overcome vast challenges. In one case, an official was discreet about not embarrassing a mother who had faked her child's birth certificate by altering a photocopy of another birth certificate. The fake document was of course not accepted, but the mother was nonetheless treated with dignity. Several administrators went out of their way to be helpful and respectful to community members by taking time to explain very carefully what they knew or to be flexible about allowing a family to relocate before obtaining a certificate of detention for an incarcerated relative.

Unfortunately, when one agency prepares families for departure while another agency prepares for their arrival, the miscommunications can be significant; for example, some families were told they would receive $400 each on arriving at the site, only to discover after moving that they would have to wait an undetermined time to receive any money. A few administrators were lacking in respect and seemed to be playing by their own rules. We are troubled by occasional situations when administrators withheld information from community members in order to save spots on a resettlement list for their own relatives, or were perceived by community members as behaving "with hostility," which prevented people from ques-

During one of ATD Fourth World's Community Forums, a Tulay resident
explains the commute from Manila to the Calauan relocation site.

tioning them. In one case an administrator said, "I will choose who will
be on the lists in order to send thieves and others with a bad reputation to
the most distant site. Don't try to help anyone with a bad image or it will
create a bad image for others you know." While this statement troubled us,
it is absolutely not government policy, and we see that the vast majority of
administrators are doing their best to make the resettlement process work.

Overall, however, the relocation process has been highly administrative and has lacked the flexibility to take families' concerns into account.
Our efforts to ensure that families could receive correct information and
express their preference among the available sites had very little impact.
In theory, an appeals process exists for community members who are
unhappy with their assigned sites. However, the process seems fruitless
for two reasons. First, it cannot create new slots when the existing ones
are no longer allocated for residents of Metro Manila. And second, it consists mainly of administrators insisting that the families' documentation is
incomplete, even when we know that everything was submitted correctly
but then misplaced by one of the agencies.

Schooling — and hunger

By the end of 2014, during which eighty-four of the families we followed were resettled, the contrast between the priority families and the stronger ones was starker than before. These differences were clearly due to the greater economic difficulties of the priority families. Lack of income, hunger, and school attendance were inextricably linked. While resettlement does offer better housing, the priority families have so far not been able to thrive in other areas of life. Their children attend school even less often than when they lived in Manila. The lack of possibilities to earn a living makes hunger a significant problem. In Manila, families could often sell small items by walking up to vehicles stuck in traffic on the highway. The low population density in the new sites means that so far only the most dynamic families have been able to succeed in commerce.

In the stronger families, all the school-age children attended school before the relocation, and the move disrupted schooling for only 6 percent of them. In the priority families, 54 percent of the children did not attend school even before leaving Manila. Following the move, most of those who had been attending school stopped going, leaving 85 percent of all the school-age children in the priority families out of school.

Hunger is a principal reason that some families no longer send their children to school after resettlement. The priority families worry about sending their children to school hungry, knowing that hunger will keep them from learning. They also now live in a place where the walk to school is too long for the children to come home at lunchtime and too isolated for their children to perhaps receive a few coins from passers-by for their lunch, as they might in Manila. They also know their children will feel shame at not being able to bring a snack to school. So if, in the morning, they do not have food to give their children to take to school, they are likely to keep them home.

The lack of income and food has been documented by others as well. Following a large wave of resettlements in 2005, the Philippine Center for Investigative Journalism reported: "Many of the evicted families now face starvation as they have been relocated to places far from where they work and where there are few jobs available. [...] With no money and no income, residents are stuck here, facing the specter of starvation."[17]

---

17. Pabico, Alecks P. "Thousands of evicted families go hungry in resettlement sites," *Philippine Center for Investigative Journalism*, October 4, 2005.

Children in Norzagaray enjoy a book during our literacy program, Ang Galing.

Nine years later, the situation remained difficult. In late 2014, Anne-Sylvie Laurent wrote: "Of the thirty-four families we know who have been re-settled, at least ten families suffer daily from hunger. Even though their neighbors' solidarity ensures that they can eat at least once a day, hunger and lack of livelihoods are the main reasons people return to Manila." In another report, she recounted a conversation between two mothers:

N: *The other day I received a sermon from the workers of the religious group here. They told me that I can't just come and ask for rice. I don't like doing this, but we had nothing at all really. Sometimes I send the children.*

E: *The time before that, we went together. She received food, but not me because they said they can give to only one. It's only here that the children have learned to drink coffee with sugar instead of eating a meal. My daughter asks me, "What will we do, we have no food?" In Manila, we have a lot of strategies to put food on the table, but here we can't.*

N: *You know, I often smile, but not always. Sometimes I cry when I see what our meal is.*

It is not only hunger that keeps resettled children from getting an education. For children who do attend school, challenges remain. Another member of our team in the Philippines, Vanessa Joos, notes, "Some children feel discouraged from attending school since teachers call them 'bobo' (stupid)."[18] A Peace Corps volunteer described some of the challenges at one resettlement site: "Only twelve teachers work at the school, though two thousand kids show up here every day. They work ten-hour teaching days, teaching classes of sixty or more children in two shifts, morning and afternoon. [...] There were only a few [teachers] in the entire community who had graduated from high school."[19] In some sites, to lower the class size to a maximum of fifty-seven students, teachers work twelve-hour days teaching three shifts: 6 to 10 a.m.; 10 a.m. to 2 p.m.; and 2 to 6 p.m. Anne-Sylvie noted, "The principal of two schools in one relocation site is very alarmed about the number of new students and how the teachers will be able to cope. She said, 'Even if we repair old rooms to use them as classrooms, we lack physical space. They relocate families but don't coordinate with us.'" In the Pandi site, the 700 residents of the original village are now far outnumbered by more than 300 resettled families. The enrollment at the nearby elementary school has quadrupled, so they, too, will begin teaching in shifts in 2015.

Before the resettlements, some families were receiving scholarships from private non-profits for the costs associated with public schooling. While there are no direct fees, families must pay for uniforms, shoes, notebooks, and food. In addition, some homework requires internet access, available for a cost in cybercafés. Some classes ask families to contribute to the cost of school projects or to replace an electric fan in the classroom. And when schools are not within walking distance — as is the case for most secondary schools — there are costs for transportation. However, most of the scholarships that the resettled families used to receive are reserved for children in specific districts, and are thus lost when a family moves.

---

18. Rodriguez, Fritzie. "Sleeping above tombs and living among the dead," *Rappler*, August 21,2014.

19. The Peace Corps–Philippines. "Resettlement Project," "Pioneers! O Pioneers!" *Blog*, July 21, 2010.

A family makes time to read and learn together as part of our Ang Galing program. Challenges to schooling in the relocation sites include hunger, class size, and lack of materials and space.

It is hard to send teenagers to school when they can earn something elsewhere. A 14-year-old told Anne-Sylvie that she did not transfer to the school in the relocation site and was managing to earn a little bit of money. Anne-Sylvie noted, "With her, it is difficult to speak about school or no school, for this year or for next year. She is already behind for her age. Will she be able to resume school next year? I will ask her and her mother, but I have many doubts that this will be a priority for her family in the coming weeks because they have other worries. […] Another mother tells me that her daughter is too shy to go back to school, knowing that she would be with younger children because of the schooling she has already missed. She has often begged for alms at the traffic lights. […] Although she is under 18, the chicken-packing factory has hired her. The chemicals used there attack the workers' skin."

In the midst of demolition, a resident explains
the limited choices available to families in poverty.

Another member of our team, Guy Malfait, wrote after a visit to a different relocation site, "Y., who is almost 13, is not happy to be here. He would prefer to be back where he has friends and where there is food." Other teenagers feel the same way. Especially in the evenings and on weekends, they find the resettlement sites boring. The great distances, even between different sections of a single site, and the cost of transportation prevent them from discovering what is around them. Guy continued about Y.'s family:

His mother says he's not motivated to go back to school. He's too shy because of his age. And she also needs him to watch the younger kids because she's hoping to get a job washing dishes at an eatery. They have tried returning to Manila, but they say the police chase them away. To have her son end up in detention is what she wants to avoid at all costs. Her two youngest were sick with fever some days ago. She is worried about her own health too, and has asthma. She said, "I cannot die yet; you see I still have small children." Tomorrow she will turn 33, but she's already thinking of dying! [...]

I also had a long talk with a grandmother who explained that her granddaughter is not enrolled this school year. The woman cannot read or write and feels ashamed about it. She is praying that her granddaughter will be able to learn. [...] I spoke to a woman who has put her children into a shelter for three months.

She says, "It's true they are not children who live in the streets, but I'm alone and I need to have a job. What do you want me to do? Leave them alone when I'm out working? Who will take care of them? What will happen to them?" A father next door who is listening says, "Never, never. My children are the most important thing in my life." As the woman continues to explain, her neighbor softens his words. He, too, must know that most of the time the choices of poor people are too limited.

Income and livelihoods

Eviction is devastating in the moment but also has a demonstrated lasting impact on families. Research in the United States on the long-term effects of eviction on women shows that the challenge of earning money is likely to last: "The year following eviction is incredibly trying for low-income mothers. Eviction spares neither their material, physical, nor mental well-being, thereby undermining efforts of social programs designed to help them. [...] We found that the impact of eviction on some outcomes may be stubbornly resilient, enduring years after families were forced from their homes. We found some evidence that, at least two years after their eviction, mothers still experienced significantly higher rates of material hardship and depression than their peers."[20]

The situation in Manila is no different. In 2014, the priority families as well as the stronger ones found it difficult for an entire family to remain together in the resettlement site. Not a single one of the priority families has been able to earn money in the new site. About 80 percent of both groups had a breadwinner return to Manila. For the priority families, 67 percent of the ones who returned took the whole family back to Manila, compared with only 19 percent of the stronger families. The stronger families were more often able to remain in the settlement sites because 16 percent of them were able to earn money there, and in some cases both a husband and a wife did so.

The subsidies from DILG (Department of the Interior and Local Government) can be an opportunity for more dynamic families to invest in

---

20. Desmond, Matthew and Rachel Tolbert Kimbro. "Eviction's Fallout: Housing, Hardship, and Health," *Social Forces Advance Access*, February 24, 2015.

Frequent traffic over the bridge in the Tulay community allowed
many residents to earn a living by selling food or other items to
people in the vehicles, as Mr. Rolando does here.

starting a small business of some kind: driving a pedicab, or selling food
or other items out of their home or from a bicycle. But the priority families
struggle much more. Planning anything, much less the establishment of
a business, is a challenge because, in some cases, people learned only the
day before their relocation that they would receive $400 in cash. Others
who expected a subsidy learned only on arrival that they might not in
fact receive it. Having counted on the money, they had no assistance at
all to start over.

Some families who *did* receive the subsidy discussed it with our team
and decided that the team could function as an informal savings agent
for them, keeping their money in Manila and visiting regularly to return it to them when they need it. But the distance involved made other
families too anxious to leave the money in Manila, realizing that in an
emergency they would not have the means to travel back to retrieve it
and would have to wait until the team's next visit or ask a member of the
team to make the trip especially to bring the money. At the same time,
one of the mothers said, "You know, we are always hungry here. How
do you want me to stay away from the box with money and not to get it

out? When you don't have money, you don't have it, but when it's within reach you cannot stay away."

Anne-Sylvie wrote, "We sat with them several times during the following weeks to discuss their ideas of livelihoods, how they were doing, how they budgeted, etc. But this did not lead to success because of lack of knowledge of the new surroundings and lack of potential clients. Just a month after their resettlement, there is a high risk that their hopes for their livelihoods will fade — not vanish, but fade."

On a visit to families in the Norzagaray resettlement site, Anne-Sylvie noted that because the site is on a hill, transportation by pedicab is difficult. Also, the market and the school are so far from residents' homes that transportation is a daily expense. Guy asked two women how they were managing:

A: *If your husband has work in Manila, when he comes back here the money is just used to pay the debts.*

O: *I sell vegetables and soup. I travel every day to buy them in the market. But sometimes I don't sell everything because people have no money to buy. And yet it's important to go every day to the market because there is no refrigerator to keep things cool.*

Guy: *If you go every day, could you buy also for the others, so several of you share the cost of the transportation?*

A: *It's not possible. She is old and would have difficulties carrying everything. Also if she is the only one buying she might buy something wrong or forget something. [She can't read,] so we cannot make a list for her.*

One of the fathers in the stronger resettled families earns money as a pedicab driver. However, he does not earn much because he does not own the pedicab. He is also fined if he pedals beyond his assigned zone, even though he feels he cannot refuse to take a client to a requested destination. His wife previously worked as a domestic in the Middle East, but she found it difficult and returned. Now she hopes to find domestic or care-giving work in Manila. It is hard to start a business in a place that is sparsely populated, like the Norzagaray site. It has capacity for two thousand families, but only three hundred lived there in September 2014, when the site was closed to other families from Tulay who requested it.

The resettlement site in Norzagaray.

Water is expensive and must often be pumped and carried. In Norzagaray, although a reservoir is being built to make water available throughout the day, water was available only twice a day when families first moved in. Electricity is also expensive. In the Pandi site, families are limited to using a single light bulb, one fan, and one television. Refrigerators are not allowed at all because of their high energy consumption, even though they could help a person who sells food to store unsold items for another day.

Some of these families benefit from the national cash transfer programs of the Department of Social Welfare and Development (DSWD), which include grants for education and health, and also offer skills training. While living in informal housing in Manila, some families were eligible for Modified Conditional Cash Transfers (MCCT) for one year. They may then be transferred to the mainstream cash transfer program called Pantawid Pamilyang Pilipino Program (the 4Ps). There are eight administrative requirements for each family to get the 4Ps, and the criteria and procedures are sometimes unclear. Guy notes, "Families borrow money to pay the expenses of the requirements. How strange that you need to have money in order to prove that you're poor enough to be part of the program." Once they have transitioned to the 4Ps and their folders are transferred to the new municipality, if they leave the new site to return to Manila, they are likely to lose their 4P grants too. At the same time, they continue to be summoned to certain meetings in Manila to receive the grants and to participate in sessions teaching skills and values. The beneficiary families who have already relocated are often notified very late about these meetings, for which they need to pay transportation to attend. While both cash transfer programs can provide families with invaluable support, there can be problems as well. Rappler social news network reported:

> *[Two mothers] made sure that they followed the rules [...] to remain in the program. [Neither wanted] to lose one of the most helpful things in their lives then, just like the other mothers in their community. However, problems began to emerge as early as the first month when they were supposed to receive their pay-outs from the DSWD. The money they were supposed to receive in February 2013 was released two months later. They resorted to borrowing money just to be able to eat every day. [...] Once they finally receive the money, a huge part of it goes to paying debts they incurred during the months they had no resources. [...] The problem with the MCCT worsened when the payouts stopped in September 2013. According to one*

A resident in the Tulay community uses the heat of a candle to seal the plastic packaging of snack food that he will later sell on the bridge. At the relocation sites, there is little opportunity even for such small ways to earn money.

mother, their current contract was supposed to run until December of the same year. Her co-parent leaders contacted the local DSWD office only to be given vague answers to their questions. [...] She said, "We're always given dates, only for them not to [follow] through."[21]

In May 2014, the MCCT payments had not resumed. One of the parent leaders of the Tulay community frequently contacted the office to ask for information, and was told only that she was too demanding. The parent leader reacted, "If they would tell us we won't have the money, at least we would know. But they say nothing. Why do we get no information?"

Claude Heyberger is part of ATD Fourth World's regional team for Asia. Thinking about livelihood possibilities for relocated families, he wrote, "We heard of jobs proposed for further construction of the site. It seems the information is brought door-to-door by local authorities, so one problem is for people who are in Manila all week long — how will they hear about it? Another problem is for people like one father, now 51, who doesn't feel that he has the strength anymore to work on a construction site. The only work he knows is selling things on the roadside in Tulay. The poorest people are not the ones able to catch such job opportunities near the sites. And for some sites like Pandi, there is really not much around."

Solidarity among families

During the commemoration of the World Day for Overcoming Poverty in October 2014, several community members spoke about supporting one another:

Loretta: *We know well how to pay back our neighbors for help we receive: when we have no money, we give rice or onions, or we propose services, such as getting water at the pump for them.*

Mariafe: *All of us here in the relocation site get a share when there is a little 'blessing' that arrives, even if it's only little. Somehow we manage to get by.*

---

21. Gavilan, Jodesz. "Families living under Quirino Bridge strive to survive," *Rappler*, June 4, 2014.

Lucio: *It feels good to help. In our community we are used to helping each other. Based on our experience, it is easier for us to get help from our poor neighbors when we are in need than from the rich.*

Gina: *All of us help each other, not only financially but also by giving good advice.*

While such mutual support and friendship have long existed in every informal settlement, being split into five resettlement sites makes it harder to help one another. One mother notes, "My friend's house is far away, but when one of us asks for help, we are there for each other." It is particularly important to invest time in maintaining relationships and building new ones because the newcomers in resettlement sites are not always made welcome. People who have been there longer may say: "They are a different kind of people. They don't behave like we do. Sometimes they are hot-headed or shout at each other."

The Community Forum dynamic run by our team fosters mutual support among families who are coping with different levels of poverty. It also

Some two hundred families lived on this pier amid shipping containers before being resettled. Now far outside Manila in areas like Balagtas, they appreciate the housing. However with no ways to earn money, they say, "We get hungry and we take on debts."

creates a mechanism for resettled families to begin building connections with their new neighbors. Young people within each community show their solidarity with children by supporting our different cultural and educational programs. Our team reaches out to young people from priority families as well as the more dynamic ones in order to train them for this. The young people offer a keen knowledge of the children around them and the realities of life in their communities. Adult community members, as well, often approach our team to point out that another family needs support to meet requirements for the resettlements.

Taking stock in January 2015

There are still seventeen families remaining in the Tulay community under the bridge. Twelve of them are priority families, and six of those families are returnees who will have to move without benefiting from the resettlement program. In Navotas, where 192 families used to live on a pier covered with shipping containers, all but one have been resettled.

North Cemetery, 2014: Women making traditional
Christmas stars during a Community Forum.

Calauan site, November 2014: Mr. Christopher, formerly of Tulay, and Ms. Lita, who lives in the North Cemetery, construct a Christmas star.

On six different dates between April and December 2014, eighty families from Tulay were resettled. They were split among Calauan, Balagtas, Norzagaray, and Pandi. Claude observes:

> *There is something people appreciate in these sites. Almost all of them try to find at least a small way to make things look nice and homey. The inner walls of bare cinder blocks are sad, so one young woman is painting one flower on each block of her father's home. Some neighbors have joined together to start gardens in the common spaces. […] One family whose children used to beg on the street in Manila has been able to take on responsibility in their resettlement site, where others chose them as "block delegates" to represent them in meetings with the district chief.*

Anne-Sylvie notes, "It is actually nice to see families we know in a house. One parent told me with a big smile, 'Now I will use the bathroom!' Less than an hour after arriving, some families had installed their television and were sitting together to watch and to chat. […] However, these families are just at the beginning of the adjustment stage, trying to find a new balance in their lives."

One mother says, "Every time I go under the bridge, I'm reminded that I'm a squatter. To have a real house makes me feel normal like other citizens. I want to have flowers in front to make it beautiful." But despite having left the bridge in 2014 to be resettled, her family did not manage to stay in the resettlement site for more than a few weeks. Because the only place they can earn money is along the highway in Manila where her

North Cemetery, 2014: Reflecting and writing together during a Community Forum.

husband sells bottled water and crackers, they have returned there together. A round trip for a single person between Manila and their relocation site costs the equivalent of four kilos of rice; they cannot afford the travel and are again reduced to being squatters.

Some of the resettlement buildings are already deteriorating, and the challenge of finding work must be faced. In the Norzagaray site, Guy observes, "On this visit, I see that the holes in the roofs have been repaired but whenever there is wind, the galvanized iron sheets blow up and down like they are not well fixed. Every strong wind tears new holes." During a visit to Balagtas, where sixty-five thousand people have been rehoused, several families met in a Community Mini-Forum. Before resettlement, they used to live in Navotas, hemmed into narrow passageways between and beneath shipping containers stacked six high where, families said, "It stank. It was dark, and it used to flood often. Many of us got sick there." They prefer Balagtas because "it is quiet here, with water and electricity." But they also say, "There is no income here, so we get hungry and we take on debts."

None of the families who live among tombs in the North Cemetery have yet been eligible for resettlement. However, as our team continues to run projects in the cemetery, adults hear news about the resettlements. Some of them have traveled to Calauan to facilitate children's creative workshops. They have a growing interest in requesting and preparing for a good relocation site for their community. One mother in the cemetery said, "The government is doing so much for informal settlers now. Why could we not be part of it? We don't want to miss the opportunities. But we know it would be very hard for us to move far away because our livelihoods are here in or near the cemetery. Here, the people know where to go, what to do to find even small jobs. A relocation site should have all the facilities we need: a school, a health center with a doctor, a market, and opportunities to earn a living. How can resettlement really be an opportunity?"

Cristina Lim-Yuson, who served as president of ATD Fourth World in 2009–14, spoke about the families who were resettled, saying how much they need friends "to stand with them through the most difficult and challenging times and to support and strengthen the families' determination to live in dignity. There is a difference in the quality of living under the bridge and in the relocated sites. There is fresh air and some land to till and plant. Mothers are no longer afraid that their children will get run over by the speeding buses and 'jeepney' vans in Manila. But definitely, survival without any livelihood strains the families. [...] I pray that we are spared from typhoons, as we experience an average of twenty typhoons a year now, a serious setback for our country. Climate change affects everyone, but especially the poorest."

Our team in the Philippines continues to offer intense accompaniment to the priority families and to accompany dozens of other families who are more dynamic. Our goals are:

- to help people see and seek opportunities in the resettlement sites and to keep hope;

- to continue learning about and understanding the many aspects of this evolving situation;

- to support children's education and adults' efforts to develop livelihoods;

- to continue building connections among community members and with other partners;

- to seek recognition of the experience of community members.

At the same time, we know that community members cannot speak out about their experience without taking risks. One mother agreed to

Ms. Cristina Lim-Yuson, president of the Museo Pambata children's museum,
plays the accordion at a 2011 Festival of Learning in Tulay.

speak with a journalist, but then said, "They must not mention our true
names or any information about us, or else it will ruin our lives." In a
project as challenging as mass resettlement, it is vital for us to learn from
the most vulnerable people about what it is like for them and how they
try to cope. And yet, the threat of negative consequences limits their freedom to speak publicly.

The Filipino government has greatly improved its approach. On the
delivery of the 4Ps, one woman says, "This year, the system has improved.
The pay-out has started again. We are offered some cash-for-work opportunities that can last for six months, such as street sweeper, salesperson,
bartender, laborer. There are still some delays in the pay-outs but it is
better than before. The cash-for-work stops after six months so that others
get a turn to earn money too. And social workers have started to register
new families who were not yet in the program."

In a heavily populated country that is losing land to global warming,
home ownership is a challenge for a majority of the population. Despite
this, and with very limited economic means, the government is now mak-

ing it possible for thousands of informal settlers to live in homes made of concrete, and eventually to own them. However, these resettlements were designed mainly as part of the plan for cleaning Manila's polluted waterways as soon as possible. Dialogue and partnership with community members have not been a priority, which means the process has been ill-adapted for the families concerned, particularly for the most fragile among them. For instance, before resettlement, the information provided by implementing agencies is brief and given only orally, meaning that many people miss it and then feel lost after moving. The relocated families are suddenly in an environment where they know nothing about schools, health care, non-profits, or programs to support them as they try to find a livelihood. Even when advance consultations were initiated by project developers, as one community member observed, "The project is already decided and framed. Even if we attend the dialogues, nothing changes about the project; we just have to follow." Once families arrive in resettlement sites, the lack of possibilities for earning money is often compounded by their unfamiliarity with a new environment they did not choose and may be afraid to explore.

Recommendations

In the Philippines and elsewhere, we recommend that future resettlements take advantage of the experience and knowledge of people who have been through previous evictions and relocations. Vanessa notes that people "already feel guilty for living poorly. The government must respect them too. [...] Informal settlers shouldn't be treated as mere beneficiaries, but as capable partners in the planning and evaluation of programs — especially when developing relocation projects. [...] Sustainable jobs are needed, not just dole-outs."[22]

Another key element to the success of the resettlements is the active role of each family. When it is possible for them to choose a site where they think they will be able to make a new life, this element of choice can help them to succeed. Anne-Sylvie observes, "When families are relocated in a site they visited and where they said that they think they can thrive,

---

22. Rodriguez, Fritzie. "Sleeping above tombs and living among the dead," *Rappler*, August 21, 2014.

"Leave No One Behind": new residents at the Calauan site display their part of the 2014 World Day for Overcoming Poverty slogan.

it does have a positive impact. One family was immensely disappointed not to be able to go to one specific site. Following a visit to that site, the wife had remarked to her husband, 'There, we could use our pedicab to do recycling.' But they were relocated to another site further uphill and far from recycling job possibilities. They are trying to make it work, but so far they are not thriving. Things could have been hard in the other site too, but a door this woman once imagined as open has been slammed shut by the change of site."

By involving community members as active partners at every step of a project, it will be possible to improve the process for everyone. Future resettlements should draw on the knowledge of people who have past experience of evictions and relocations, and should include the following:

- Higher awareness that different levels of poverty co-exist within a single community. The specific concerns of fragile and dynamic families alike must be taken into account in order to ensure that resettlements can be positive for all of them.

- Throughout the consultation process, written information, images and descriptions of available sites, and written minutes of the meetings should be made available and left for future consultation at nearby local government units.

- In advance of the move, site visits should be organized for relocating families to provide them with specific, comprehensive information on finding work and basic services so they can plan their new lives in advance.

Keeping hope: Despite hunger, schooling, and livelihood difficulties,
resettled families start common gardens and help organize cultural and
educational activities. Above, families in the community of Balagtas
come together with artist Robert Alejandro to decorate.

- Community members should be allowed to move to the sites they
  choose as most appropriate for their family's needs, and where
  they think they will thrive.

- Outreach should guide and support people who do not know how
  to apply for the administrative documents required to relocate.

- Job training should be offered to reinforce existing and potential
  skills that fit any opportunities to earn money in the relocation site.

- After resettlement, support and guidance should continue in order
  to ensure that families can access schooling and basic services.

- Transportation should be provided for people who need to return
  to their previous communities to earn money until they can
  develop another livelihood in or near the relocation site.

• Community solidarity should be supported through regular meetings among newly relocated families, existing community members, and other stakeholders such as non-profit organizations.

All these measures should be regularly evaluated together with the people living in persistent poverty who have been affected by the resettlements. When any families are left behind, it is crucial to understand the reasons in order to adapt current resettlements to their needs and to improve the design of future resettlements.

• • •

In our collective blog, our Manila team shared an exchange with one of the men who was resettled in 2014:

"No comment…." That's Mr. B's reply when I ask him about the situation in the relocation sites. […] Last December Mr. B invited some other newly relocated families to see the small yard in front of his house. He insisted on taking a picture, saying he probably had the most beautiful Christmas decoration of the whole site. For sure, the house represents the hope for a better life. "A once-in-a-lifetime chance," he and others will tell us. The families are all very thankful for the opportunity to obtain and live in a "real" house. For most of them, it's the first time in their life.

Somehow, instinctively, they know what they have missed for all these years. Within the first hour after arrival in the new house, the families started their new life: children were playing with a ball, and a mother walked her toddler in a stroller. This they could not do under the bridge. We see the happy faces; we see the big smiles; we see eyes full of hope.

However, after the first hours or days of ecstasy, the real challenge starts. For them, to move is not just a matter of changing places; it's the start of a new life. In Tagalog there is only a one-letter difference between the words for life (buhay) and house (bahay) but, better than anyone else, Mr. B and all other relocated families know what a difference a letter can make.

"No comment…" was probably a very wise reply. Mr. B, too, hopes that a new house will be the start of a new life, but he couldn't

just say this. Too many uncertainties were probably still in his head. Will he find a job nearby? Will his children get enrolled in school? Will he be able to pay the monthly utility bills and mortgage of the house?[23]

ATD Fourth World is impressed with the vast scope of the challenge facing the government and all the implementing agencies involved in these resettlements. However, as recommended above, there are several important factors to address. Involving some of the most vulnerable adults in the planning and evaluation of the resettlement would be a significant way to address Mr. B's uncertainties, to begin closing the gap between the priority families who have already been relocated and the more dynamic ones, and to avoid such gaps for those yet to be resettled.

---

23. ATD Fourth World–Philippines. "Relocated Families Look Back on Their Situation," *Together in Dignity collective blog*, February 19, 2015.

3

Human Rights in Guatemala, Thailand, and Peru, and at the United Nations

Guatemala — Doña Nicolasa Lopez Cruz is an activist[24] who lives in the 18th zone of Guatemala City: the Colonia Lomas de Santa Faz. This is a neighborhood where exclusion is worsened by inequality of opportunities. The community suffers from the plague of crime linked to gangs. One day a gang member attacked a young man working for a cable television company who was circulating to collect payment from customers. The gang member pushed this young man up against the wall of Doña Nico's home while shouting threats to kill him unless the man gave the gang member all the money he was carrying. Doña Nico came out of her home and began talking to the gang member. She had known him since he was a child and urged him not to kill the young utility worker. She spoke to the gang member of his childhood and of his own suffering. She said she understood his aggressive behavior, but reminded him that he was better than this behavior and that he could still choose not to continue attacking the young man. Doña Nico understood that the gang member needed the money he intended to steal, that he had a family to support, and that it is hard to find work when you did not succeed in school and when problems have piled up over the years. But she explained to him that the young man was a hard worker supporting a family and that he should not die. In the end the gang member let the young man go.

Doña Nicolasa Lopez Cruz.

24. Fourth World activists are people who live in extreme poverty and make efforts to defend others and to work to claim their collective rights.

In a neighborhood where many people live in fear, often locking themselves indoors to avoid problems, not all of us know how to create peace in the way Doña Nico did: coming outside to confront a young man and prevent him from hurting another by reminding him that he could still make the right choice.

On another occasion, Doña Nico intervened in her neighbor's family. The neighbor, a single mother raising teenage girls, works in the city's largest marketplace, called the "Terminal." From 6 a.m. to 6 p.m., she earns only 60 quetzales (about $8 US), which has to cover the family's food and household expenses and her daughters' schooling. Sometimes the mother just cannot manage any more and becomes aggressive toward her daughters when they disobey her. When this happens, Doña Nico intervenes by preventing her neighbor from doing anything she might regret later. Doña Nico tells the neighbor that when she can no longer handle things, it would be better for her to leave her daughters until she feels calmer: "Sometimes I feel that way too. I get fed up! But beating our children isn't the solution; it changes nothing; it only makes things worse."

Doña Nicolasa (seated, at center) with other ATD Fourth World members in Guatemala, at a stand displaying fair-trade products they designed and created.

To us, Doña Nico has said, "My neighbor needs help. She had such a hard childhood, and she just can't face her troubles alone." Doña Nico does not judge her; nor does she justify her behavior. Her approach is to get involved to prevent any harm to the daughters, while offering her own support to the neighbor to avoid new difficulties. Like so many other people we know who live in poverty, Doña Nico is an artisan of peace: not the semblance of peace where people hide behind walls and don't get to know one another; but peace that enables each person to develop fully, to enjoy a decent life, and to be taken into account.

Another one of our activists, Doña Raquel Juárez has for many years now been on Guatemala's Committee for October 17, World Day for Overcoming Poverty. She noted, "The poorest people are never recognized for their virtues or their sacrifices. What about the virtues of so many mothers who care for their children despite the hardships, so many young people fighting for a place in a society that

Doña Raquel Juárez.

turned them down before they had even begun, so many men who, even when they are humiliated, don't lose courage and keep working day after day to earn only a pittance?"

That is the importance behind October 17, the World Day for Overcoming Poverty, when people living in deep poverty around the world are recognized for their unrelenting struggle to exercise their human rights as well as for their role as artisans of peace. This recognition is not for professional and personal accomplishments, but for each person's inalienable dignity. This recognition is also why we strove to have October 17 in Guatemala linked to its national Rose of Peace.

The "Rose of Peace"

The Guatemalan Civil War lasted for 36 years (1960–96). Strong and lasting peace accords were finally signed on December 29, 1996, between the Republic of Guatemala and the Guatemalan National Revolutionary

Don Oscar López Ramirez
changing his country's
White Rose of Peace at the
Guatemala Peace Monument
on October 17, World Day for
Overcoming Poverty.

Unity, which comprised four opposition guerrilla groups. One year after
that date, a sculpture was inaugurated: the Peace Monument and White
Rose. The sculpture shows two hands pointing skyward, having just released a dove of peace and freedom; the dove, not shown, is represented
by a fresh white rose, which is changed during a special daily ceremony.
By placing a fresh rose on the monument every day, Guatemalans demon-
strate their commitment to the peace accords and their hope for lasting
peace.

Those first invited to place a fresh rose on the monument and to
make a public statement were public figures or representatives of non-
profits working to promote development and peace. Currently, the rose
is changed by a distinguished visitor or by people nominated beforehand
to the National Peace Secretariat for their professional and personal accomplishments. These people are named "Peace Ambassadors."

For the changing of the white rose on October 17, 2012, to recognize
the efforts for peace made by people living in poverty, the secretariat chose
one of our members, Don Oscar López Ramirez. In his message that day,
he said, "Peace begins in our families, as we teach our children to live in
peace. But there's no peace if our children go hungry because there's no
work to be found. We are searching for peace, but we do not live in peace,
because we go through harsh times. Our dream is of a true peace for our

nation, and beyond it, for the world. I think that work must be shared with the poor because we know that we can work; you can trust us."

People, treated as "inhuman" for centuries

For centuries and in every society, individuals, families, and peoples have been left to endure extreme poverty, isolated and abandoned, during times of crisis as well as during important moments of human advancement. Lasting deprivation condemns people to mere survival: it forces them to focus on immediate concerns, jeopardizes their plans for the future, and compels them to make impossible choices: Should the day's meager income go toward food or toward children's shoes? Should a parent with no safe place to leave children while working simply hope for the best or lock them into their home in hopes of protecting them? Lasting deprivation separates families and forces them to compete for resources that are always in too short supply. But people say, "The worst thing is the contempt; they treat you like you are worthless; they look at you with disgust and fear; they even treat you like an enemy, like we were not even humans." The callous treatment takes many forms: disrespect, humiliation, discrimination, and insults culminating in physical violence suffered by people in extreme poverty at school, at work, or in the street. "It wasn't just that I had nothing, but that I had been reduced to nothing," said one parent who is homeless.

People living in poverty regularly experience denials of their dignity and equality. Living in poor neighborhoods, they have little access to quality education or health care, the demands of survival leave them little time to participate in the lives of their communities, and the frequent acts of humiliation undermine their self-confidence. Thus, poverty becomes entrenched and passes from one generation to the next. They are confronted by severe obstacles that prevent them from enjoying their rights and assuming their responsibilities as parents and citizens, all of which undermines their self-respect and perpetuates their poverty. They are trapped by "powerlessness, stigmatization, discrimination, exclusion and material deprivation, which all mutually reinforce one another."[25]

---

25. Office of the United Nations High Commissioner for Human Rights. Guiding Principles on Extreme Poverty and Human Rights, p. 2.

A course of action advocating
the recognition of everyone's human dignity

Joseph Wresinski launched a course of action to encourage everyone to defend the human rights of all people. When in July 1956 he first arrived in the emergency housing camp of Noisy-le-Grand, France, where he would later found ATD Fourth World, he was struck by the dimensions of the destitution there and its links to people in other places and times throughout history — people trapped in workhouses or threatened with jail for begging. The need for a bold course of action hit him like a lightning bolt:

> *The sun was scorching and the alleys were deserted. There was no one outside. In front of this emptiness, I said to myself, "In the old days, sources of water, road junctions, churches, or business brought people together. Here utter poverty is what has brought people together." [...] The families gathered there should not be seen as individuals side by side, or a cluster of "social cases," as the administration and charitable organizations believed then and still believe too often. [...] Walking alongside a poverty-stricken people, we wanted to place them boldly in today's history, [...] to see a*

1966: Emergency housing camp of Noisy-le-Grand, France,
where Joseph Wresinski founded ATD Fourth World.

Participants learning about and standing up for human rights
at a 2007 People's University in Cuzco, Peru.

historical identity [rooted in exclusion and inequality] where others
were denying that this was a social reality. [...] Since then, I have
been haunted by the idea that these people would never escape
from their poverty as long as they were not welcomed as a whole,
as a people, in those places where other people held debates and led
struggles. They had to be there, on equal terms, in every place where
people discuss and make decisions not only about the present, but
also about people's destiny and the future of humanity.[26]

Wresinski's course of action was to focus on actions that would help
people to enjoy all their human rights and to assume their responsibilities. Little by little, an increasing number of the people he worked with
started to express themselves and to participate in the civic life of their
communities, towns, governments, and international organizations. From
1956 on, activities, events, meetings, and festivals were organized to promote respect of human rights for all people as a priority for everyone.

---

26. Anouil, Gilles. *The Poor Are the Church: A Conversation with Fr. Joseph Wresinski,*
Founder of the Fourth World Movement. Twenty-Third Publications. Mystic, CT, 2002.
Pages 48-49.

At various periods and in various places, ATD Fourth World's projects have focused on literacy, cultural education for children, the People's University,[27] access to decent work or to health care, or on a comprehensive approach to ending homelessness. All of these projects have at their core the goal of promoting respect for the human dignity of each person, and ensuring her or his enjoyment of all human rights without exception, in equality, without discrimination.

Throughout the 1970s and '80s, the international human rights debate was highly polarized by the Cold War: some countries were proud of defending civil and political rights, while others spoke of the primacy of economic, social, and cultural rights. In this context, one man living in extreme poverty in France voiced his frustration during an ATD Fourth World conference: "Everyone here is protesting the exile of Andrei Sakharov in the USSR. It's good that they are. But the same people don't lift a finger to defend a family in complete misery who are holed up in a concrete bunker built during the war, right down the road from Versailles!" During those years, Wresinski continued to denounce extreme poverty as a violation of all human rights, as serious as racism or torture — but public opinion of the era did not take him seriously.

Appealing to the United Nations and the world

In May 1982, ATD Fourth World initiated a petition asking the United Nations to recognize extreme poverty and social exclusion as violations of all human rights. At the time, extreme poverty was considered an issue to be addressed by charitable or humanitarian aid, not a question of human rights. Two years later, 300,000 signatures had been collected from people from all backgrounds all over the world. They were presented to UN Secretary-General Javier Pérez de Cuéllar, who then recommended that the UN Human Rights Center (now the Office of the High Commissioner for Human Rights) collaborate with ATD Fourth World on this issue. This petition began a long history of consultations, including participation in working groups, meetings, seminars, and sessions.

---

27. The People's University is a regular discussion forum for people in poverty to talk freely with one another and to engage with people from other walks of life in mutually respectful dialogue. See Volume 1 of this publication for more detail.

1984: UN Secretary-General Javier Pérez de Cuéllar receives from Joseph Wresinski 300,000 signatures declaring extreme poverty to be a violation of human rights.

A decisive event ensued in February 1987, when Wresinski addressed the 43rd session of the UN Commission on Human Rights (now the Human Rights Council). He presented an official French government report that he had written on extreme poverty and economic and social insecurity.[28] With concrete examples of the life of very poor population groups around the world, his presentation demonstrated the interdependence and indivisibility of all human rights, and the fact that extreme poverty represents a violation of these rights, be they civil, political, economic, social, or cultural. Wresinski appealed to the Commission to examine the question of extreme poverty and human rights together with people whose rights are not respected, and with them to develop an understanding of the indivisibility of all rights.[29] Leandro Despouy, then the ambassador of Argentina to the United Nations,[30] recalls hearing Wresinski speak:

28. Adopted by the French Economic and Social Council: "Grande pauvreté et précarité économique et sociale."

29. Wresinski, Joseph. *Refuser la misère, une pensée politique née de l'action.* (Paris, Editions du Cerf, 2007.) Pages 209-214.

30. Since then, Leandro Despouy co-authored a report on human rights abuses committed against the extrajudicial captives detained by the United States at its naval base in Guantanamo Bay, Cuba.

Mr. Leandro Despouy speaks at a 2008 international colloquium about the impact of Joseph Wresinski's thinking.

He already had an important reputation. He spoke very naturally and told us, "If you do not understand that extreme poverty is a serious violation of human rights, you understand nothing of human life. The time has come for the poorest to enter the United Nations, which cannot live by hiding the reality of deep poverty." He did not speak with arrogance, but he questioned us strongly. He asked, "What are you doing? You speak all the time of violations of rights, but you are by-passing the major problem." It's true that the international context was difficult. At the time, questions of extreme poverty were not linked intellectually with human rights. There was even a certain fear of raising the subject because wealthy countries refused to recognize the existence of poverty within their borders and, by the same token, communist regimes could not admit that poverty was present in their countries. As for the Third World, the countries were stigmatized.[31]

In 1989, at its 45th session, the Commission on Human Rights adopted its first resolution on Human Rights and Extreme Poverty, asking a sub-commission to examine the feasibility of carrying out a study on extreme poverty and social exclusion with the participation of people living in poverty. That was the beginning of many subsequent consultations with people living in extreme poverty, governments, human rights experts, and others — and of voluminous reporting by UN Special Rapporteurs on this topic, including Leandro Despouy's "The Realization of Economic, Social and Cultural Rights: Final Report on Human Rights and Extreme Poverty," written in 1996 in collaboration with people living in poverty around the world.

---

31. From Despouy's address during a December 2008 colloquium at SciencesPo, the Paris Institute of Political Sciences.

2005: Families living in poverty in Thailand give their input during consultations on international guiding principles on extreme poverty and human rights.

Elaborating new UN Guiding Principles

As a result of Despouy's report, in 1998 the Commission named a Special Rapporteur on Extreme Poverty and Human Rights, "to give greater prominence to the plight of those living in extreme poverty and to highlight the human rights consequences of the systematic neglect to which they are all too often subjected."[32] By 2001, the consultations carried out by the five experts of the sub-commission had led to a process to develop guidelines for implementing human rights standards to be used in fighting extreme poverty. A number of consultations and technical seminars were conducted with the participation of people living in poverty themselves. Governments, human rights experts, national human rights commissions, and non-governmental organizations (NGOs) were all invited to contribute to the text. In August 2006, the United Nations' Sub-Commission on the Promotion and Protection of Human Rights adopted draft guiding principles entitled "Extreme poverty and human rights: the rights of the poor."[33] In 2008, ATD Fourth World published

---

32. As set forth in a mandate available on the website of the Office of the High Commissioner for Human Rights.

33. This draft was developed by a UN group of experts headed by José Bengoa (Chile), and composed of Emmanuel Decaux (France), Asbjørn Eide (Norway), and then El Hadj Guissé (Senegal), Julia Motoc (Romania), and Yozo Yokota (Japan).

"Dignity in the Face of Extreme Poverty," a report based on consultations with people living in poverty and extreme poverty in France, Peru,
Poland, Senegal, Switzerland, and Thailand, and with NGOs committed
alongside them, including members of the Forum on Overcoming Extreme Poverty.[34]

It was highly unusual in the UN context to have consultations designed specifically in ways that enable people living in the most extreme
poverty to have a meaningful voice. Vicki Soanes, then one of the volunteers[35] representing ATD Fourth World at the United Nations, writes:

> In spite of increasing rhetoric about the importance of participation,
> the poor are largely absent from the discussions at the UN. [...] The
> poor are either subsumed into other identity groups [such as women,
> people with disabilities, and indigenous peoples], or the Non-
> Governmental Organization community is seen as their legitimate
> representative. However, such representation presents serious
> problems, and these NGOs are made complicit in the continued
> marginalization of those whom they purport to represent. They do so
> by replacing them in the debates; through the frequent combination
> of charity and advocacy, which means that the poor are less likely
> to freely express their views to their NGO representatives; through
> a lack of local political awareness such that local participation
> frequently reproduces the existing local power dynamics; and through
> the absence of, and unwillingness to hear, the very poorest in such
> consultations. Furthermore, when the poor are able to express their
> opinions, NGOs are adept at adjusting these views in order to fit
> their advocacy goals, highlighting the problem with representation
> at high-level debates. The most influential advocacy NGOs are those
> that are centralized and professionally staffed, meaning that they
> are less likely to be close to those they represent. Furthermore, the
> common assumption that Southern NGOs are closer to the poor
> is not necessarily true. Some Southern NGOs tend to have more
> in common with the elite of the Global North than the poor of the

---

34. The Forum is a network of 3,500 correspondents in 130 countries, coordinated by
ATD Fourth World.

35. Fourth World Volunteer Corps members choose to link their lives over the long-term
to those of families living in poverty.

Ms. Vicki Soanes (right) listens as ATD Fourth World activist
Ms. Emma Speaks takes the floor at the United Nations in New York.

*Global South. This is particularly the case when the organization has
a hierarchical structure and its representatives are professionals based
in Northern centers. [...] Those in power should have the chance
to meet with people living in poverty. That personal contact would
challenge preconceptions about poverty and stimulate action.*[36]

Some of our members in Thailand who live in a shantytown or under
a bridge were among those consulted by the United Nations in 2006–07.
They sleep out in the open, with no privacy and in crowded surroundings.
Only a few dogs protect them from violence at nighttime. Their informal
work includes removing seeds from peppers, collecting paper, plastic, or
glass for resale, making wreaths of flowers to sell, or cleaning the local
temple. Because they live on privately owned land in an informal community, if they want their children to be admitted to secondary school they
must find someone in another area who is willing to declare the child as

---

36. Soanes, Vicki. "Rocking the Boat. The participation rhetoric exposed: Why should
people living in poverty have a voice and space at the United Nations?" Research thesis
for the Victoria University of Wellington, April 2010.

People living in poverty in Thailand are consulted about the drafting of guiding principles to ensure human rights for all.

domiciled in their home — two years before the child finishes primary school. If the people in these informal communities get organized and take initiatives, such as arranging care for their youngest children while the parents work, they run the risk of attracting attention. Since they do not have the right to be living there, they are afraid of being evicted. Pagakaew Nuian, one of our members, explained to a UN-appointed expert, Prof. Yozo Yokota of the University of Tokyo, the uncertainty she and her neighbors endure:

2005: Professor Yozo Yokota, a UN-appointed expert on human rights, listens to families living in poverty in Thailand.

In this area, people can't make a decision to go to the district to ask for registration so we can have access to running water and electricity. People are afraid of the landlord, they're afraid of the police. They think that if we get involved like that, we might get evicted although we've been living here for a long time. Fear is one of the reasons why there is no solidarity, because our future is unsure. It's hard to make plans for the future, to build on a land that belongs to someone else. We stay like that, we don't claim anything; we just hope that we can stay here, that's all.

Another one of the activists consulted, Woranat Laithong, spoke about discrimination:

I know the social service unit at a hospital where some nurses are not very friendly. They spoke unkindly to me, and I asked if they wanted people to die on the road like dogs. When rich people come in cars, they rush to greet them. Some people in society think people here are promiscuous. What do they think of the women here? They look down on us because they see us sleeping under a bridge. It's because we are the have-nots. […] Every person has a value. Instead, they look down on us. For what reason?

In Peru, UN expert and anthropologist José Bengoa consulted friends and members of ATD Fourth World who are part of an Andean population in isolated mountain communities greatly impacted by discrimination.[37] Marleny Vargas described the disdain of one segment of the population towards indigenous culture: "When we speak a language like Quechua, we don't speak Spanish well and as a result bear the humiliation of mockery. [This happens] also because of the clothes we wear." Isabel Huamani spoke of a food assistance program intended to help mothers of young children: "People who have identity papers do not need this assistance; they run a store or work in a business. However, renters and people who struggle to make a living, who have several children, who do not have papers, and who have no place to live, gain nothing from [this program]. The people who need it the most […] receive nothing." Margarita Enciso spoke of situations where, due to their living conditions, the poorest families are not in a position to fully assume their parental responsibilities:

I started working at the age of 11 [in domestic service]. They made me sleep with the rabbits, in the kitchen, not even in a bedroom. The guinea pigs were walking across me. They gave me the leftovers from their meals. You don't even treat an animal that way. I always said to myself, "My daughters will never work as domestic servants, never. I am going to fight that." However, I was not successful, and that's

---

37. The partners in this consultation were: Asociación Civil "Gregorio Condori Mamani," Proyecto Casa del Cargador; Sindicato Nacional de Trabajadoras del Hogar; Defensorías Comunitarias; and Defensoría del Pueblo–Cusco.

Families in Cuzco, Peru, welcome their national Defender of
Human Rights for consultations on the Guiding Principles.

*why one of my daughters works as a domestic. She had to abandon
her education. We don't want our children to work either, but we
don't have enough money. Our children see our powerlessness. We
do what we can, but it isn't enough to pay for the house and school.
Therefore they help us by working.*

Still others consulted in Peru spoke of forced sterilization. When one
young child had died, nurses refused to issue the mother a death certificate unless she agreed to be sterilized. Gregoria Achircana also recounted,
"In rural areas, when women are pregnant and go to the clinic, they are
threatened with being sterilized. There have been cases where the clinics
forcibly sterilized women to prevent them from having children, and as a
result, women no longer want to go to the health center. It is a violation of the person, of the culture, and of their dignity." Others in Peru
recalled that some women, because they lacked money to pay hospital
fees, were asked by the hospitals where they had just given birth to sell
their newborn baby. The women affirmed, "Baby trafficking does exist.
Generally, they confront families of modest means and take advantage
of their situation." José Bengoa, who coordinated the UN experts' work
on the Guiding Principles on Extreme Poverty and Human Rights, was

In the isolated mountain region of Cuyo Grande, Peru, a Street Library takes place in a field, where a girl (right) holds up her favorite book.

thanked by the people he consulted in Cuzco, Peru. They explained why they appreciated his role, saying: "It is very difficult to have one's rights recognized. Primary school is free. But in the village, teachers demand that parents contribute to the parents' association. And in setting the amount of the dues, it is mainly the wealthiest parents who have a say. These dues render school inaccessible. [...] But by referring to rights, to the potential for appealing to the Defender of Human Rights [a nationally appointed ombudsperson], it has been possible to win out."

On the basis of the consultations organized by ATD Fourth World as well as extensive consultations with governments, NGOs, and human rights experts, the then UN Special Rapporteur on Extreme Poverty and Human Rights, Magdalena Sepúlveda Carmona, prepared the final draft of the guiding principles. During the Human Rights Council's 21st session in September 2012, her draft was adopted by consensus. The UN General Assembly then noted the new guidelines "with appreciation." Looking back on her 2008–14 mandate as Special Rapporteur, Sepúlveda said, "Those living in poverty were the real driving force behind the need for the

Ms. Magdalena Sepúlveda Carmona, UN Special Rapporteur on Extreme Poverty and Human Rights (2008–14), consulted several times with people living in poverty. Here, she is at ATD's January 2012 colloquium on the violence of extreme poverty.

United Nations to develop these Principles. We cannot forget that Joseph Wresinski himself pushed the UN to draw up mechanisms to protect the rights of the poor. Thanks to the work of ATD Fourth World, the poorest members of society participated in the consultations on what the Principles should cover. I must say that, for me, the contributions of these individuals were a key part of the work undertaken. When drawing up the Guiding Principles, I was able to take account of the perspectives held by those living in poverty whom I met as part of my work as Special Rapporteur. Those individuals shared with me their experiences and ideas on a wide range of issues, ranging from discrimination to social protection and ways of life."

These UN Guiding Principles on Extreme Poverty and Human Rights represent a significant breakthrough in the thinking about poverty. The text recognizes that extreme poverty is both a cause and a consequence of human rights violations — not just the result of economic deprivation. It states that governments have a legal obligation under human rights law to eradicate extreme poverty. Human rights should play a major part in tackling poverty and guiding all policies affecting persons living in poverty. The latter should be recognized as "rights holders" — people who have the same rights as everyone else — and agents of change, able to participate in all stages of developing policies and programs that affect them directly. The text thus establishes an advance over the traditional thinking that tended to consider people in extreme poverty as objects of charity or as passive recipients who deserved a minimum level of humanitarian aid. Building on the concrete experiences of persons living in poverty, governments, human rights experts, and NGOs, the Guiding Principles set out the main obstacles that prevent people living in extreme poverty from enjoying their fundamental rights, and recommend a series of specific actions to overcome those obstacles. In this way, the Guiding Principles represent a valuable tool for human rights defenders and all those who work day after day to promote human rights and eradicate extreme poverty. The text is particularly useful for persons living in poverty, as it can help them to formulate claims or complaints based on a better understanding of their rights.

However, because the Guiding Principles are written in the language of human rights texts, ATD Fourth World and other NGOs active in the fight against extreme poverty were concerned that many people would find the recommendations hard to understand. They therefore launched a project to develop a handbook for people working at the community level — whether as NGOs or for public services — to explain the implications of the Guiding Principles and put forward suggestions about the types

During 2007 consultations on the UN Guiding Principles on Extreme Poverty and Human Rights, Don Julian Quispe speaks out in his native tongue, Quechua, as a rights holder and agent of change.

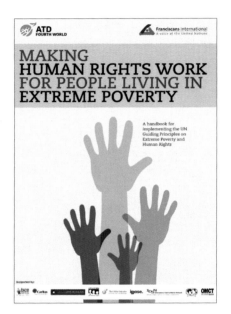

Designed by practitioners and people living in poverty, this handbook translates United Nations' principles and language into concrete suggestions for ordinary citizens to take action.

of actions that could be taken to help people living in poverty to claim their rights. NGOs working in a range of areas — on children's rights, the right to food, economic and social rights, the rights of people with disabilities, etc. — joined in on the project. The International Federation of Social Workers (IFSW), for example, with members in 116 countries, welcomed the idea of a handbook: "As community work is one of the core tasks of many social workers, IFSW is very much interested to support and promote the publication of a handbook implementing human rights standards in the fight against poverty." One of the opening chapters of the handbook is devoted to "Key principles for engaging with people living in poverty," emphasizing the importance of fostering people's genuine participation in identifying priority concerns and the types of action that they want to take to address them. The handbook, published in 2015, is a key tool in promoting human rights in ways that empower people living in poverty.[38]

---

38. Available for download at: http://atd-fourthworld.org/wp-content/uploads/sites
/5/2015/05/2015-09-01-GuidingPrinplsEPHR-HANDBOOK-EN-ATD_FI_Handbook
_English_WEB-1.pdf

Ensuring the rights of children and their families: key to overcoming poverty

Our experience has shown the tremendous importance of families in enabling people who live in extreme poverty to survive and to continue to fight against poverty. Family members can provide one another with the love, security, and support that is crucial to children's development and that strengthens all members of the family. For these reasons, in 2004, we published the results of a study called *How Poverty Separates Parents and Children: A Challenge to Human Rights*.[39] In this study — carried out in Burkina Faso, Guatemala, Haiti, the Philippines, the United Kingdom, and the United States — our members identify and examine the effects of poverty on the possibility of living together as a family. The study examined situations of foster care and adoption, centers for children living in the streets, and orphanages that often provide temporary care for children from families struggling to afford the costs of food and school fees. This work, supported by UNICEF and the UN Program on Family,

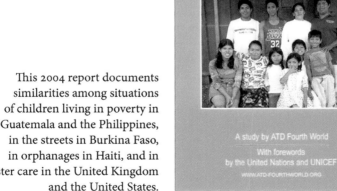

This 2004 report documents similarities among situations of children living in poverty in Guatemala and the Philippines, in the streets in Burkina Faso, in orphanages in Haiti, and in foster care in the United Kingdom and the United States.

---

39. Skelton, Diana and Valérie Brunner. *How Poverty Separates Parents and Children: A Challenge to Human Rights*. (Méry-sur-Oise: Fourth World Publications, 2004.)

Ms. Marta Santos Pais speaks at ATD's 2012 colloquium on the violence of extreme poverty.

was followed by contributions on these issues from many NGOs. In 2009, the UN General Assembly adopted a set of Guidelines for the Alternative Care of Children, negotiated over a period of five years with governments, UN agencies, and NGOs. These guidelines are grouped around two provisions: that such care be genuinely needed and that, when it is necessary, it be provided in an appropriate manner. Since the approval of the guidelines, the continuing challenge has been how to implement them. How can comprehensive strategies to support vulnerable families be developed when there are only limited resources? How can a constructive dialogue be initiated with key stakeholders? And, if family separation is being considered by child welfare institutions, how can we ensure that the child and his or her family are able to truly participate in the decision-making process?

Also in 2009, the United Nations named Marta Santos Pais as Special Representative of the Secretary-General on Violence against Children. When Ms. Santos Pais was the Rapporteur for the UN's Committee on the Rights of the Child in 1991–97, representatives of ATD Fourth World had many opportunities to consider with her and the Committee the experiences of families living in extreme poverty who have been confronted for generations with a lack of comprehensive family policies, with arbitrary foster care policies, and with pervasive abuse in residential institutions for children. She sees consulting with children as a core dimension of her mandate, and writes, "Children show remarkable resilience. They have become true agents of change, to break the invisibility of violence and to generate action and debate." Addressing members of ATD Fourth World at a colloquium in 2012, she spoke of children she had consulted in Asia who are "arrested by police or welfare services simply because they are begging in the street, [...] placed in overcrowded care institutions where they are further victimized [...] and often had their hair shaved off so that authorities would easily be in a position to recapture them. For these children, information about their rights, about protecting their existence and safety, and fighting the violence surrounding them is non-existent or not accessible. [...] I feel very challenged when I recall that the international community has identified ending extreme poverty as a priority, and has identified the fight [to stop] violence against children and young people as a human rights imperative but between words and reality there is a huge gap. You are helping us to break this silence and the invisibility of violence that surrounds the lives of those living in extreme poverty and deprivation. [...] I want to commit myself to continue so that your voice can be heard and can influence lasting change in each and every country in the world."[40]

"To come together to ensure that these rights be respected is our solemn duty"

Looking back at all the steps made to address human rights and extreme poverty, Leandro Despouy reflects:

Fr. Joseph Wresinski showed well the link between extreme poverty and discrimination. Exclusion can be due to many factors, but deep poverty leads inevitably to exclusion. Historically, governments speaking from a rights-based point of view have denied the existence of extreme poverty. Another face of extreme poverty must be found. Perhaps this is the most universal and relevant message from Wresinski's thinking: if we do not change the way we look at the poorest, it will be hard to find an adequate response. And inadequate responses sometimes worsen the situation of the poorest people. [...] I wish I had Wresinski's moral authority to be heard so that the world would consider it morally intolerable and socially dangerous

40. Brand, Anne-Claire, Beatriz Monje Barón, et al. *Extreme Poverty Is Violence — Breaking the Silence — Searching for Peace.* (Vauréal, France: Revue Quart Monde Publications, 2012.) Pages 77–78.

for the powerful and the poorest to continue navigating away from one another.[41]

The Guiding Principles on Extreme Poverty and Human Rights constitute an essential tool for institutions and nations to end the morally intolerable conditions of extreme poverty. At the same time, discrimination exists as much in personal attitudes of bigotry as in discriminatory policies. Ending social exclusion requires not only that human rights law be implemented, but also that all people come together to learn to see one another differently. This is why the commemorative stone, first unveiled on October 17, 1987, concludes: "Wherever men and women are condemned to live in extreme poverty, human rights are violated. To come together to ensure that these rights be respected is our solemn duty."

Commemorating October 17 provides opportunities for people such as Ambassador Despouy, Doña Nico, and others of all backgrounds to come together, act in solidarity, and build a culture of human rights. This commitment to dialogue has created the conditions needed for people to see and speak to one another in new ways. It has fostered a new vigilance for ensuring that not a single person's inalienable dignity is denied. Without respect for each and every person's human rights, as inscribed in declarations and conventions, no community or country can enjoy governance that is fair and equitable for all. Inversely, it is only thanks to individuals, neighborhoods, and nations that human rights are brought to life to protect and sustain the daily lives of the least powerful people. This constant interaction between legal human rights frameworks and the human commitment needed to implement them informs our approach to overcoming poverty.

---

41. From Leandro Despouy's address during a December 2008 colloquium at SciencesPo, the Paris Institute of Political Studies.

4

Taking a Country at Its Word: *Challenging Human Rights Violations in France*

Instruments such as the Guiding Principles on Extreme Poverty and Human Rights and the Guidelines for the Alternative Care of Children can mark a turning point in the history of the struggle to end poverty. However, as noted by Marta Santos Pais, even policies meant to promote human rights and participation too often remain hollow. We know that many governments and policy makers are deeply sincere in their commitments to defend each person's dignity and human rights; and we also know that in many parts of the world, countries lack the economic means and human resources to implement approaches that governments might want to take. Creating a power struggle on the issue of human rights and extreme poverty would serve no one. Our question is how to develop co-responsibility for creating positive social change.

A collective human rights complaint to the Council of Europe

The Secretary-General of the Council of Europe, Thorbjørn Jagland, strongly insists that Europe must invest in its social responsibilities to fight poverty:

> *The reality in the European Union is that there are 80 million poor people and inequality is increasing. Extreme poverty has greatly increased. We must see beyond statistics, the problem concerns real people. [...] There can be no doubt that extreme poverty is a violation of human rights. [...] There are two solutions: reinforcing our democracies and sharing social responsibilities. The framework must be reinforced by human rights. Poverty endangers social cohesion. We must reinforce democracy by giving a voice to all citizens.*

2005: Messages drawn by children near Herblay, France, to show
their solidarity and encouragement for Traveller families being evicted.

*To share social responsibilities, we must invest more in human
resources. We cannot accept reductions in social spending. The efforts
of the poor alone will not be enough. To get the poor out of poverty is
an obligation for the states. This crisis should not be used to allow for
any regression on human rights. We must concentrate our forces and
change perspectives to invest directly in our social fabric.*[42]

For decades, France has tried to invest in its social fabric by adopt-
ing ambitious legislation in order to fight poverty and social exclusion.
However, this legislation has not removed the difficulties faced by people
and families living in poverty. Taking France at its word requires using
the human rights tools it has helped develop to ensure that the legislation does not remain hollow. This is why, in January 2006, ATD Fourth
World's international president, Mr. Oguié Anoman of the Ivory Coast,
filed a collective complaint with the Council of Europe against France for

---

42. From opening remarks made by Mr. Jagland on February 13, 2013, at the Council of
Europe's conference on "Poverty and Inequality in Societies of Human Rights: the
Paradox of Democracies."

violating four articles of the European Social Charter, specifically those concerning the right to housing. This filing was possible because of a 1994 modification to the French penal code. Previously, only individuals were allowed to bring cases charging that they had been discriminated against. The 1994 change, which followed extensive lobbying by ATD Fourth World, gave non-profit organizations the right to bring cases on behalf of individuals living in "social or cultural exclusion due to their condition of extreme poverty."

Mr. Anoman's 2006 complaint cited situations of homelessness and discrimination against Traveller[43] families long settled in the Val d'Oise district but never included in housing development plans, despite repeated requests to the municipality to address their lack of decent housing. In 2004 the township of Herblay had legally evicted the Travellers' trailers from land they had occupied continuously for twenty to thirty years. The Travellers' appeal was refused in 2005 and they were instructed to pay a fine of 70 euros a day until they vacated the site. Most of them scattered and were repeatedly evicted from a series of other sites in the district, with disastrous consequences for their children's schooling.

Herblay, France: One of the sites from which
Traveller families were evicted.

43. Travellers are "a community of people who are commonly called Travellers and who are identified (both by themselves and others) as people with a shared history, culture, and traditions including, historically, a nomadic way of life" according to the Pavee Point Traveller and Roma Centre.

Also cited in the complaint were families of Yenish[44] origins in Alsace, living in dilapidated former military barracks and in damaged trailers beside an airfield, with no clean water, sanitation, or electricity. Settled there since 1964, these families had applied for housing in the district. Beginning in 1994, ATD Fourth World supported their applications, gradually gathering additional support from neighborhood associations and local citizens. Only in 2000 did the district provide one faucet of drinking water for the 84 people near the airfield. Three years later, the district finally proposed a location where housing could be built for them — but this proposal offered only one site, which the group had long requested avoiding. The site already housed another group of Romani origins, and the first group feared that old rivalries might surface. No other site was proposed.

The experience and analysis of people living in poverty was the basis for this complaint. In September 2007, a delegation of 37 members of ATD from across France were allowed to directly address the European Committee on Social Rights — only the third time in history that such direct testimony took place. Speaking for the delegation, Cécile Reinhardt said:

> *Ladies and gentlemen of the jury, we place great hopes in this collective complaint. I've lived half my life in insecure housing. How can we live as citizens without living fully with rights? When can we tell our children, "You'll live in decent housing"? I am making this complaint for us but also for all the poor.*

Although no progress was made on that day, Cécile was not discouraged: "As small as we are, we were able to come here to be heard."

An initial response from the committee, in June 2008, reminded France of its obligations concerning the right to housing of people living in situations of extreme poverty, calling on France to apply "in a determined and ambitious manner" standards on access of settled Travellers to land. The committee's final decision, on February 27, 2010, pertained to both Travellers and Romani peoples. The decision noted that France

---

44. Yenish, also called "gitans" in French, are the third-largest population of nomadic Travellers in Europe. The Yenish people have lived in Western Europe for more than 300 years.

had deprived these families of their right to housing and thus caused their social exclusion by failing to provide living sites with decent conditions for sanitation and security of occupancy. This unanimous decision concluded that France had failed to respect the European Social Charter and had caused discrimination.

As a result of this decision for the families in Alsace, the outdoor site was paved so that rain no longer leaves them mired in mud. Some modern housing has been built, but not yet enough for all. The families evicted from Herblay were offered subsidized apartments, which some were glad to move into. However, those who prefer living in trailers as a way to maintain their culture have still

Ms. Cécile Reinhardt: "How can we live as citizens without living fully with rights?"

not been able to find a permanent site. The under-prefect in the city of Argenteuil (also in the Val d'Oise) finally agreed to meet with these families in person, and a public study was initiated to explore a solution. The most constructive result of the 2006 complaint was that it enabled all the families named in it to be recognized as rights holders, first of all in their own eyes, and also in the eyes of the authorities. The European experts on social rights showed them great respect and attention when they presented their case. The original complaint, and other similar ones, also contributed to France passing a law in 2008 guaranteeing subsidized housing to any legal resident who cannot afford a decent home.[45]

In making this collective complaint, our hope was to shape a unified dialogue among all the institutions playing a role in the lives of families in poverty. Only through this unified dialogue can existing social policies and human rights law be applied in the way they were intended. In

---

45. This is called the DALO law, for "Droit au logement opposable," passed on January 1, 2008.

fact, some French administrators told us that our collective complaint was helpful for them as well, because it created a framework to address situations that had frustrated them. A collective complaint may not be the most appropriate way to unify dialogue in every country, but in France this approach made it possible for everyone to move forward together. Evaluations of policies and laws must consider not only whether they have been adopted but also what their concrete results are for people living in extreme poverty. If the most vulnerable people are not involved in how rights are implemented, and if their situations are not the reference point for measuring the efficacy of these rights, then social discrimination will only worsen.

Challenging poverty-based discrimination

Looking for housing is so hard. Even if we can pay, they only show us squalid, substandard housing.
> — Quentin

Some real estate agents have clear instructions from landlords. They are not to offer housing to certain classes.
> — Gerald

At the hospital, a person came to make an appointment. Her insurance card is the CMU[46] one. The secretary said in a loud voice, "You are with CMU, so you can wait longer for the appointment." This person was humiliated in front of everyone in the waiting room.
> — Laurence

I used to work as a nanny for an important public official. One day he learned that I had grown up in foster care. He was angry that I had not told him this when he hired me. He told me that I couldn't be trusted and that he could no longer leave his children with me. So I lost my job.
> —Noémie

(From testimonies written for the World Day for Overcoming Poverty, Metz, France, October 17, 2013.)

---

46. Couverture médicale universelle: a government plan reserved for the unemployed or anyone who has difficulty getting regular insurance.

• • •

Classism — defined as prejudice or discrimination on the basis of social class, which can be expressed through individual attitudes and behaviors or through a body of policies and practices — continues to harm people living in poverty, preventing them from enjoyment of their human rights. In 2013, ATD Fourth World–France launched "No More," a petition to the French government and Parliament denouncing instances of classism:[47]

- Children of the unemployed were refused access to school cafeterias on the grounds that their parents should have time to pick them up and make them lunch;
- Some mayors decided that offering public housing would be dangerous because of the residents' poverty, or they legislated against begging, camping, or scavenging;
- Some doctors refused to treat patients insured by the CMU;
- Children were insulted as "welfare kids" in school because of their parents' need to rely on public assistance;
- Landlords refused to rent to families based on their physical appearance, despite their ability to pay the rent;
- Job applicants with skills equal to others were discriminated against for living in emergency shelters or having addresses in low-income areas;
- Visitors to a museum were made to leave "because other visitors had complained about their smell";[48]
- Barbers in a shop refused to cut the hair of a homeless man.

"No more," a 2013 petition asking the French government to ban discrimination on the basis of social exclusion.

<hr />

47. In French only: "No more: Petition for the recognition of discrimination on the basis of social exclusion." ("Je ne veux plus: Pétition pour la reconnaissance de la discrimination pour raison de précarité sociale.") ATD Fourth World–France. 2013.

48. Gordts, Eline. "'Smelly' Family Kicked Out Of Paris' Musee D'Orsay." *The Huffington Post*: January 29, 2013.

Unfortunately, such examples are only too numerous. A city bus driver in eastern France slowed down at a stop where just one woman was waiting, then sped up again without picking her up. The woman phoned the bus company to complain and was told that the bus driver said, "When I saw such a badly dressed woman, I thought she was poor and a drug addict, so I didn't stop."

In another situation, Véréna Caffin, a member of ATD Fourth World, lost a close friend in April 2013.

Ms. Véréna Caffin.

He was a person who had no money, but a heart of gold. He opened his door to me when things were not going well at all. He hosted me when I found myself homeless. He gave me the desire to continue living when everything was dark for me. For me, he was more than a brother, more than a friend, more than a father. I don't know if there's a strong enough word to really say what he meant to me....He was buried in the indigent section of the cemetery — that is to say directly in the ground. I didn't want that for him, especially after all he had done for me. The day before the burial, we went to the funeral home to view him. We were asked to return at 4:30, so we did. I wanted time for a viewing, time to reflect. But it wasn't possible: the body was already in the hearse and wouldn't be moved before the funeral the next day. The hearse was in a parking lot, at a distance from the funeral home. My friend had to spend his last night out in a parking lot where anything could have happened.

Classism, racism, and "de facto apartheid"

ATD Fourth World has long argued that discrimination based on the perception of class (sometimes called "povertyism" in the United Kingdom) constitutes …

[…] a barrier to people moving out of poverty […and] perpetuates a lack of knowledge and understanding about the lives of people

experiencing poverty. Such attitudes are sometimes based on the view that people living in poverty are inferior or of lesser value. The consequence of povertyism, for those who experience it, is that such attitudes become a driver of a particular policy approach that results in denial of their human rights.[49]

As noted in Volume 1 of this book, the term "Fourth World" comes from the "Fourth Order," coined by Dufourny de Villiers in 1789 in an early effort to alert France about social and political discrimination against people in extreme poverty. We chose this as part of our name to raise awareness about discrimination and exclusion.[50]

For awareness to be raised, it is important for people to have opportunities to get to know one another, both within low-income communities and throughout the various sectors of society. However, Bruno Tardieu, director of ATD Fourth World–France, points out, "A phenomenon is growing: the fragmentation of disadvantaged communities. People in poverty are increasingly alone. They work irregular hours, one hour here, one hour there, often by themselves. There are no longer as many ways to be part of a collective work force or to be reached by a union. Due to budget cuts in recent years, there are fewer neighborhood gathering places, such as community centers, settlement houses, and community colleges." Furthermore, as people become more isolated, it can create discord and conflict when a country has terms and standards for only certain kinds of discrimination when another one, based on poverty, is also very present:

[In] France's 717 "sensitive urban zones," most of them in the [low-income city outskirts...], unemployment is over twice the national rate. More than half the residents are of foreign origin, chiefly Algerian, Moroccan, and sub-Saharan African. Three-quarters live in subsidized housing; 36% are below the poverty line, three times the national average. In 2005, after three weeks of rioting that ended in a government-imposed state of emergency, there was talk of a "Marshall plan" for [these zones....] Manuel Valls, the interior minister, who cut his teeth as mayor of the multicultural

---

49. Davies, Matt. "The effects of discrimination on families in the fight to end child poverty." Joseph Rowntree Foundation. November 2008.

50. Grenot, Michèle. *Le souci des plus pauvres: Dufourny, la révolution française et la démocratie.* Rennes, France: Presses Universitaires de Rennes. 2014.

[low-income] district of Evry, talks of de facto "apartheid" in France. Over 70 different nationalities, and many faiths, crowd into [the] Sevran [district]; new migrants from Africa's poorest corners are joined by more recent arrivals from Spain and Italy.[51]

Here, as everywhere, people face multiple forms of discrimination based on gender, disability, age, language, ethnic origin, religion, or sexual orientation. The growing diversity in France compounds the sense of isolation in places where people work alone or have irregular hours. Extreme political parties exploit the alienation that pits people against one another. Tardieu adds:

If a kid is insulted at recess with a racist insult, he can shoot back, "You're racist!" But when kids are bullied for being "welfare kids" or "shelter kids," there are no words to defend them. This is why words are so important. Journalists lately have been writing about "anti-poor racism" — but those aren't the right words either. The word racism has a specific meaning. What we need is an additional word for naming the discrimination that is experienced by people in poverty.

Mr. Bruno Tardieu points out French society's lack of ways to speak about poverty-based discrimination.

In addition, to address the fragmentation of communities, we need to create common experiences. When people are isolated, they can remain unaware that they have rights at all. Many French citizens whose rights are violated — like those with CMU coverage who are turned away by doctors — don't take any legal steps to defend themselves. There are also rights that people do not dare exercise. Some 70 percent of the people who are legally entitled to the Active Solidarity Income benefit

---

51. "France's troubled suburbs — Forgotten in the 'banlieues': Young, diverse and unemployed," *The Economist*. February 23, 2013.

(meant for both the unemployed and low-wage workers) do not even apply for it, partly because they are afraid of being stigmatized, and partly because they are discouraged by administrative obstacles meant to prevent fraud. Finding a name for discrimination based on poverty and creating common experiences together will help shape the conditions necessary for overcoming ethnic conflict and for respecting all people's rights.

Seeing every young person as a chance for society

It was young people living in extreme poverty who inspired ATD Fourth World to argue for a law against poverty-based discrimination in France. In 2010, when we invited young people to speak out about their lives, their anguish at being stigmatized stood out powerfully: "The way people look at you can kill you inside," they said. They called on the prime minister and on European institutions to work against classism and "to see every youth as a chance for society." Their appeal resonated with the French national High Authority for the Struggle against Discrimination and for

Metz, France, 2013: Young people lead the way
on the World Day for Overcoming Poverty.

2012: At a national conference on poverty and exclusion,
Ms. Djemila Mahmoudi (left) and Ms. Micheline Adobati (right)
speak about the stigmatization caused by poverty.

Equality (HALDE). That same year, the HALDE asked ATD Fourth World to write a report and to present it at a hearing on discrimination. Our report focused on six different situations, including that of a homeless family who was refused housing by a landlord despite having a government stipend to pay rent. The family's children were being bullied in school because of bigotry against "shelter kids" or "social parasites." The HALDE reacted to the report and hearing in a written deliberation asking both the government and the Parliament to examine ways to fight "discrimination based on social origin."[52]

In December 2012, the government organized a National Conference against Poverty and for Social Inclusion. Ten members of ATD Fourth World were invited to be part of the seven working groups that prepared this conference. During its panel on "Changing the Way People Look at Poverty and Exclusion," Djemila Mahmoudi and Micheline Adobati

---

52. HALDE deliberation n° 2011-121, April 18, 2011.

spoke before Prime Minister Jean-Marc Ayrault. They described the stig-matization caused by poverty, which they feel is slowly weighing them down "until we no longer dare to look anyone else in the eyes." During the conference, the issue of CMU insurance was raised. When some doctors refuse to treat people insured by the CMU, it discourages others with the same entitlement from trying to seek treatment. It was suggested that sanctions be introduced against doctors who refuse to accept this government-provided coverage. Since the conference, the French Council of the Order of Doctors has asked ATD Fourth World to work on the question of discrimination against people insured by the CMU. France's Defender of Rights[53] and the government body charged with adminis-tering the CMU have invited professionals, including the Council of the Order of Doctors, to collaborate on both the development of legal sanc-tions and a definition of "refusal of treatment" to be used in health ethics guidelines. This is a positive change that, once put in place, will encourage people in poverty to seek health care without fear of being turned away.

Research: Can poverty-based discrimination be proven?

While the 2012 conference had other positive outcomes — such as a recalculation of the social welfare payment — no measures were taken concerning poverty-based discrimination. Realizing the importance of developing a legal framework to address this issue, ATD Fourth World collaborated with the research center ISM Corum[54] to investigate whether poverty-based discrimination could be measured. Together, we con-ducted an experiment from April to July 2013. Eight hundred test re-sumés were mailed out requesting work as supermarket cashiers. All "ap-plicants" were in their 30s, had similar vocational qualifications, and had recently held long-term jobs related to the positions for which they were applying. Half of the resumés also included two indicators of poverty: a current address in a temporary housing shelter; and previous employment

---

53. In the role of national ombudsperson, the Defender of Rights protects citizens from the government and has special prerogatives to promote children's rights, the fight against discrimination, and respect for ethics by the police.

54. Inter-Service Migrants: Center for Observation and Research on Urbanism and its Changes.

in a social enterprise designed to hire people having difficulties finding employment. (Through these "social enterprises," the French government grants partial funding to for-profit businesses so that they will hire and train those who have been unemployed long term.) The resumés showed that this job had been held at least seven years prior to the time of the application and had been followed by other long-term employment. The control group's resumés did not have these indicators of poverty. Applicants who had at one time had difficulty finding work and who were currently living in a shelter were found to be at a disadvantage. Resumés in this group received job offers 50 percent less frequently. The net discrimination rate for applicants whose resumés implied poverty was +30 percent in total, +25 percent among men, and +35 percent among women.[55]

Marie-France Zimmer, one of our members with firsthand experience of poverty, said:

This proves we're not liars. […] To defend ourselves against everything we hear about ourselves and about immigrants, it's important to be able to refer to official studies and figures. You can't imagine how important this is for us.

Indicateur de discrimination nette (définition B.I.T.)					
	Parmi les paires de candidatures ayant reçues au moins une réponse positive...				Indicat
	Une seule réponse positive, en faveur de la candidature de référence (A)	Une seule réponse positive, en faveur de la candidature contenant des éléments de précarité sociale (B)	Réponse positive pour les deux candidatures	Total	Taux de discrimination nette (A) - (B)
Ensemble des paires de candidatures sur offres avec au moins une réponse positive (98 des 320 offres testées)	30,6%	25,5%	43,9%	100,0%	-5,1%
paires masculines (44)	25,0%	25,0%	50,0%	100,0%	-0%
paires féminines (54)	35,2%	25,9%	38,9%	100,0%	-9,3%
offre dans un métier du nettoyage (35)	25,7%	25,7%	48,6%	100,0%	-0%
offre dans un métier de la restauration (44)	27,3%	27,3%	45,5%	100,0%	-0%
offre dans un métier de la vente en boutique (1	47,4%	21,1%	31,6%	100,0%	+26,3%

Statistics that help prove poverty-based discrimination occurs:
a snapshot from the report, "'We're Not Treated Like Everyone Else':
Discrimination and Poverty."

---

55. The detailed report of this research, available in French only, is entitled, "On n'est pas traités comme tout le monde": Discrimination et pauvreté. ("'We're Not Treated Like Everyone Else': Discrimination and Poverty.") ATD Fourth World and ISM Corum. 2013. 72 pages.

In August 2013, law professor and researcher Diane Roman published an in-depth article on discrimination based on social conditions. She placed the work done by ATD Fourth World and others in the context of French legal history, drawing on precedents in Canadian provincial laws, particularly in Quebec and Ontario.[56] She was interviewed on this issue by the French National Consultative Commission for Human Rights. The French Defender of Rights has asked ATD Fourth World to organize a training session for the law and mediation professionals he supervises throughout France on how to recognize discrimination based on social conditions.

National conference: "Be poor and shut up!"

In September 2013, together with the Defender of Rights and the National Consultative Commission on Human Rights, ATD Fourth World registered a formal request to Parliament for the existing law against discrimination to be amended to include the criterion of social conditions. At the same time, we launched a campaign to influence public opinion. In reaction to the many accusations against people in poverty that had cast a shadow on the previous election cycle, we published a handbook and designed a social media campaign — "Enough with False Ideas About the Poor and Poverty" — to refute stereotypes and prejudice.[57] That October, to mark the World Day for Overcoming Poverty, ATD Fourth World–France

A booklet printed as part of a social media campaign to refute stereotypes and debunk poverty myths.

---

56. Published in a law review in French only, under the title, "La discrimination fondée sur la condition sociale, une catégorie manquante du droit français." ("Discrimination founded on social conditions, a category lacking in French law.") Recueil Dalloz. August 1, 2013. Page 1911.

57. Sarrot, Jean-Christophe. *En finir avec les idées fausses sur les pauvres et la pauvreté.* Paris: Éditions de l'Atelier, 2013.

Caen, France: Signing the national petition, "No More,"
denouncing instances of poverty-based discrimination.

launched the petition "No More," calling for recognition of discrimination based on social conditions. More than forty other non-profit organizations joined in this campaign as partners. In December, a year after the 2012 national conference against poverty, the Minister for Social Affairs and Health organized a second conference — "Be Poor and Shut Up!" — the first ever to focus on poverty-based discrimination. By the end of 2014, the petition had collected 25,000 signatures.

An important step forward was taken on January 14, 2014, when the French Senate ratified a National Assembly decision to add a twentieth criterion to existing discrimination law: one based on place of residence. The law, now inscribed in the penal code, calls for:

> *[...] equality between women and men, policies of integration and struggle against the forms of discrimination victimizing inhabitants of disadvantaged neighborhoods, particularly as linked to a place of residence and to a person's real or imagined origins.*[58]

---

58. Law n° 2014-173 of February 21, 2014, on City Planning Urban Cohesion.

From now on, people may file charges if they believe that, because of where they live, a job or housing application has been rejected, for example, a merchant has refused to take a check, or a bank has been unwilling to provide services.[59]

The remaining challenge is to add a twenty-first criterion making unlawful any discrimination on the grounds of social conditions. The deputy minister for the struggle against exclusion has said she is in favor of this criterion. The prime minister's Secretary-General for Government has called on all ministers to express an opinion on adding this criterion to the penal code. While the law has not yet been amended as of July 2015, these steps have led the French National Assembly to agree to take the question under consideration. The minister of justice is studying draft legal language for an amendment to the law.

While the progress so far results from the efforts of many individuals, institutions, and non-profit organizations, we feel that particular credit should go to people like Cécile Reinhardt, as well as to Quentin, Gerald, Laurence, Noémie, and all the young people living in poverty who dared to speak out about painful personal situations in order to help their nation live up to its ideal of equality for all. As with the collective

Not "shutting up": In 2013, for the first time, the French National Assembly welcomes a delegation of people living in poverty.

---

59. Article in French only, "Discriminer les habitants de zones sensibles devient illégal." ("Discriminating against inhabitants of sensitive zones becomes illegal.") Zappi, Sylvia. Le Monde. January 15, 2014.

Ms. Marie-France Zimmer at the December 2012 government-sponsored conference, "Changing the Way People Look at Poverty and Exclusion."

complaint on housing, our question about discrimination is how to develop co-responsibility for creating positive social change. Pierre-Yves Madignier, president of ATD Fourth World–France, explains that the aim of pursuing changes in the discrimination law is not to launch a wave of lawsuits:

> *The goal should be to provide civic standards for each person, to play a role in educating everyone about living in a community, and to ensure that a child who is bullied as "trailer trash" can know that this behavior is condemned.*

Naming and condemning this behavior is an important step toward healing the hostility rooted in alienation and isolation. Our hope is that never again will anyone have to feel that "the way people look at you can kill you inside."

5

Horizontal Governance:
Making Choices Together and Keeping Promises

A human-rights approach is not a policy handed down from above, but a process based on the agency and free participation of all people. Everything we undertake requires creating the conditions for people whose agency has been truncated by poverty to develop their own voice and to be able to engage with others: by choosing to make commitments to one another and to seek out those who are the most isolated; and by developing new ways to think and work, to create and act together, and to live in peace together across diverse communities. To defend human rights, we must develop ways to share responsibility for rigorously evaluating and planning our work.

Evaluating and planning

"How can things ever change so that our children need not suffer as we do?" The urgency of effecting and measuring change has permeated our work from the beginning. Wresinski felt that it was work we owe to ourselves because we are determined that our actions

"Tèt ansanm" is an expression in Haitian Creole meaning that people "put their heads, hearts, and arms together" in solidarity. It expresses the way we try to share responsibility horizontally among all members of ATD Fourth World. This patchwork quilt was sewn in our Learning Co-op in Appalachia (USA).

Some of the portraits of people living in poverty who take action to improve their communities, highlighted in the video webdoc "Unheard Voices: From extreme poverty to social change."

be meaningful and constructive as we support people living in extreme poverty in their struggle for social justice. Our evaluation and planning dynamics lead to *Common Ambitions*, written together as a responsibility shared by all our members, both locally and collectively through deliberations involving every ATD team around the world.

In recent history, promises of justice, freedom, and equality for all have not been lacking. Such promises are written in great founding texts such as national constitutions and the Universal Declaration of Human Rights. There are also the strong commitments that the international community makes at historic moments, such as the Millennium Declaration in 2000 when 189 heads of state affirmed their resolve to eradicate extreme poverty from the world. Other kinds of commitments are made when catastrophe strikes, as after the 2010 earthquake in Haiti when many people, agencies, and organizations responded in solidarity. What evaluation do our societies make of the ways these promises are kept or not, of how they transform laws, policies, and life together? How can they be held accountable? And to whom? Are societies aware that these promises are not kept for everyone?

This last question is of particular concern to us. Our main focus is to engage with others as a movement through *Common Ambitions* that reflect our specific priorities, commitments, research, and innovative actions for social change. These ambitions are a contract between families living in situations of the most extreme poverty and abandonment, and others who choose to commit themselves to work with our movement: individuals from any walk of life as well as local, national, and international institutions, both private and public. These partners may be universities, businesses, artists, labor unions, educators, or non-profit organizations, to name a few. In evaluating our work and writing these ambitions, we focused on the question: "How have families confronted with the most extreme poverty gained in freedom, responsibility, and solidarity?"

Evaluating and planning together enable us, while faced with difficult situations:

- to strengthen our conviction of the meaning in our work and to give us courage despite a context of daily life that can be endlessly chaotic and blighted by violence and by troubling current events;

- to verify our focus and the effectiveness of our actions so that we can readjust in ways that allow our different strengths to complement and reinforce one another;

- to work in partnership with non-profit organizations, academia, professionals, and policy makers.

Evaluating always means looking back both qualitatively and quantitatively. But, when quantifying, it is important to choose which numbers have the most meaning for us. In evaluating a Street Library, for example, our commitment to the pedagogy of non-abandonment means that the overall numbers of children who participated matter less to us than the numbers of children who were particularly hard to reach and yet

A Street Library in Peru. Even when a program seems "successful," we still must ask ourselves who is missing and what it will take to reach and involve them.

In some 40 videos on http://www.unheard-voices.org, people in poverty express how they effect change in their own lives and those of others.

managed to join in. We ask ourselves: How many children were missing from today's activity? How many times do we need to invite an isolated family before their trust is strong enough for them to agree that their children can participate? How far might we have to walk to reach out to one specific child who may face too many daily challenges to be able to come to a Street Library?

In 2007, after many years of experimenting with different approaches to evaluation and planning, we launched an international dynamic that resulted in our *Common Ambitions* for 2008–12, which were written with more extensive dialogue among teams in many countries than any of our previous planning documents. In each team around the world, we evaluated our actions and reflected on the most burning questions we faced. Then, by combining use of the internet and face-to-face dialogues with people living far from electricity and modern technology, we were able to have exchanges among groups and teams worldwide that shed light on the choices we faced. These exchanges took place in Malagasy, Mandarin, Swahili, and other languages, and key excerpts were translated into English, French, and Spanish. In March 2008, one thousand of our members participated in these virtual and face-to-face dialogues. In previous evaluation and planning processes, a diverse cross-section of our members shared co-responsibility for rigorous collective reflection in every country and region. The 2007–08 large-scale mobilization among all of us worldwide made it possible for each of our teams to shift their perspectives thanks to questions and ideas they heard from other continents. In 2013, we published a new set of *Common Ambitions*, included in an appendix at the end of this volume.

A question we often hear, from funders and the general public, is: "How many people do you help to get out of poverty?" Effecting meaningful change in the lives of people in extreme poverty is one measure of our evaluation. However, it is inextricable from our aspiration to effect meaningful change in how society looks at and engages with people struggling to survive. Overcoming poverty requires change from people of all walks of life and from all institutions, so attempts to influence attitudes and approaches are also part of our evaluation. These questions keep us humbly challenging our action so that its driving force remains thinking, deciding, and acting together starting from the life experience of those who remain the most excluded from participation in society. By asking these questions, our movement as a whole is able to continue learning, both from people in extreme poverty themselves and from all those in society who try with constancy and sincerity to shape a world with "freedom from want and freedom from fear."

It is natural to feel outrage upon discovering the inhumanity of extreme poverty and social exclusion. This emotion, and the urgency of finding solutions, can lead people or organizations to make promises without having taken full measure of people's situations or of the kind of commitments that will be required to effect change. Their outrage can short-circuit their hope of helping. When young volunteers first joined Wresinski in an emergency housing camp near Paris in 1964, he cautioned them:

> *It should be noted that the most serious of ills that can befall a person — particularly a person in extreme poverty — is the broken promise, the unfeasible project, the pledge betrayed. Without a doubt, it is sometimes quite difficult to take stock of what might be possible in the future, but if we set out to aid our neighbors, then it seems to me that we must follow through with them on our promises.*[60]

This conviction prompted regular evaluation and planning work by all ATD Fourth World's teams, which over time has developed into a process that enables populations in poverty to participate effectively in designing the evaluation and measuring how well or how imperfectly promises have

---

60. In French only: Wresinski, Joseph. *Ecrits et Paroles aux Volontaires, Tome 1: 1960-1967,* Paris: Editions Saint-Paul/Editions Quart Monde, 1992.

Burkina Faso: ATD Fourth World members discuss their contributions
to our participatory evaluation of the international community's
Millennium Development Goals.

been kept. Creating this process in itself represents a positive ethical and
practical change for society: people who in the past felt that their existence
mattered to no one become able to play an active role in shaping their own
future and to collaborate with others in contributing their intelligence and
experience to society.

Collaborating internationally
on evaluation and planning

ATD Fourth World is neither a top-down hierarchy nor a bottom-up
federation of national associations. Our approach begins with the realities
lived by people in extreme poverty in many countries and by those who
take action alongside them. Our goal is a collective learning process in
which our teams everywhere can continue innovating in their specific
local context and at the same time draw on a wealth of experience from
other places. Our overall governance is designed to be closely tethered to
grassroots situations while keeping the big picture in view. This involves
both broad exchanges and small focused dialogues mixing experiences
at local, national, and international levels. It draws not only on the experience of those struggling to overcome the hardships of poverty, but also

on what ATD Fourth World learns from academia, from interactions with professionals working in low-income communities — educators, social workers, community police, and others — and from policy makers, such as those at UNICEF, the United Nations, and elsewhere.

In 2013, to evaluate our 2008–12 *Common Ambitions* and to choose new ambitions, we worked in several stages to spur international exchanges and reflection.

Worldwide long-distance exchanges: On four continents, 78 ATD Fourth World teams or groups joined in exchanges conducted in local languages such as Creole, Quechua, Tagalog, and many others. The goal was not only to share information, but also to think through with one another the challenges faced in the different places. After evaluating its action locally, each group prepared a preliminary paper that briefly described its project and the context of daily life in its area. In these papers, each group also put forward one question about which it was most concerned at the time. Based on this, each group was put in touch with three or four others that had similar questions, but coming from different contexts, countries, and continents. After reading one another's papers, the groups reacted to them and exchanged ideas. In addition to enabling every group to work on a question it chose and to learn from experiences elsewhere, this step created a list of the issues that were most important to our teams at the time. These issues included:

- the conditions needed for genuine participation by people in extreme poverty;

- the situation of people experiencing long-term unemployment and of exploited informal workers in the global economy; and

- how to ensure that none of our projects fall into a routine with the same participants instead of continually reaching out to people in the worst situations of poverty.

Examining our past together: Since 2008, ATD Fourth World has carried out different kinds of evaluations and participatory action-research projects, beginning with "Extreme Poverty Is Violence — Breaking the Silence — Searching for Peace" (2009–12), in which one thousand people participated. This led to a 2012–14 evaluation of the impact of the UN's

In the rural village of Mirantão, Brazil, children plant a vegetable garden as part of the school's and parents' efforts to highlight local skills and reinforce community values.

Millennium Development Goals, using participatory research conducted by two thousand people in more than twenty countries and documented in *Challenge 2015: Towards Sustainable Development that Leaves No One Behind.*[61] A video project, entitled "Unheard Voices," highlighted the role of people living in poverty in improving their communities in Belgium, Brazil, the Democratic Republic of the Congo, Haiti, the Philippines, the United States, and elsewhere. Work done on a smaller scale included:

- a participatory evaluation of ATD Fourth World–Quebec's People's Universities, conducted with academics;

- several evaluations of ATD Fourth World's impact over two decades or more in specific places in the Central African Republic, Guatemala, Reunion Island (an overseas department of France, east of Madagascar), and elsewhere;

- a session organized to examine ATD Fourth World's presence in rural communities in Burkina Faso, Peru, the United States, and other places;

- "Dreaming Permit": a collaborative artistic creation on the outside walls of a housing development, adjacent to a city demolition permit for the building, in Noisy-le-Grand, France.

---

61. Paris: Charles Leopold Meyer Foundation for the Progress of Humankind, and Fourth World Publications, 2014.

Quebec, Canada: Pooling knowledge with
academics to evaluate the People's University.

More than forty readers in different countries and of different backgrounds examined documents related to all the above projects, as well as other sources such as a UN report on Education for All, a speech by the president of the World Bank about eradicating extreme poverty, and a note by an economist at the International Monetary Fund about his work in a country in crisis. Some of these readers also read all the preliminary papers and follow-up notes from the worldwide long-distance exchanges. Based on all these documents, the readers wrote 128 short papers highlighting:

- evolutions in society and in situations of poverty;

- progress made in the work of ATD Fourth World and its partners;

- ways that our previous *Common Ambitions* should be adjusted or changed; and

- challenges ahead.

Finalizing the choice of *Common Ambitions* for 2013–17: Based on all this work and on dialogue among the readers, ATD Fourth World's

ALL TOGETHER IN DIGNITY

ATD Fourth World's Common Ambitions for 2013-2017

In Great Britain, members of ATD Fourth World say "NO" to extreme poverty.

In the USA, ATD Fourth World's team in Gallup, New Mexico develops actions in the field of education and culture with families experiencing poverty, reaching mainly Native Americans but also other population groups. Once, a volunteer noticed a couple and their baby sitting outside a food store in Gallup, looking as if they were living out of a shopping cart. He reached out to them by going over and starting a conversation. One of the first topics these parents spoke about, sitting on the sidewalk that first day, as people walked by and handed them money or food, was wanting to find ways to support their child in his development. The relationship grew over the months, as the team accompanied them in their search for housing and obtaining birth records, clothing and supplies for the baby, trying to give them opportunities to pursue whatever seemed most important to them for their future. The mother said, months later, that different agencies were willing to help them as long as they fit their criteria and accepted their "solutions." "You guys are there for us. I know that wherever we go, whatever we decide, you're still with us."

Gaps in living conditions between people struggling against extreme poverty and others continue to grow. In recent years, major ongoing crises--environmental, economic, political, and others--have hit populations in extreme poverty the hardest, reinforcing the human rights violations families in poverty already suffer. The violence of extreme poverty, ignorance, deprivation and contempt isolates people and locks them in silence to the point where they doubt that they are part of the human community. But families in poverty have experiences and knowledge that are important to share and which our society desperately needs.

And yet, too often, society's attempts to respond to extreme poverty, whether by running emergency shelters or through large-scale international aid, are planned with almost no consultation with the people this aid is intended to benefit. Our work evaluating the Millennium Development Goals showed that if the poorest are not consulted in every step of a planning process, these initiatives won't reach them.

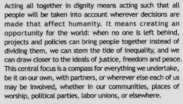

OUR CENTRAL FOCUS
Reaching Out to Those Whose Contribution is Missing

Acting all together in dignity means acting such that all people will be taken into account wherever decisions are made that affect humanity. It means creating an opportunity for the world: when no one is left behind, projects and policies can bring people together instead of dividing them, we can stem the tide of inequality, and we can draw closer to the ideals of justice, freedom and peace. This central focus is a compass for everything we undertake, be it on our own, with partners, or wherever else each of us may be involved, whether in our communities, places of worship, political parties, labor unions, or elsewhere.

We Must Ask Ourselves:

• Does our team or group work together and support one another to reach out to those who are still missing, welcoming new participants even when we lack the capacity to include a greater number of people?

• How can these people find their place and the freedom to express themselves and to contribute alongside others to our programs and projects?

• How can we link to and learn from other organizations who are also working alongside people struggling against extreme poverty, and how will people in poverty be able to enter into dialogue about the future of our world, at the local, national, or international level?

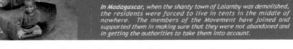

In Madagascar, when the shanty town of Lalamby was demolished, the residents were forced to live in tents in the middle of nowhere. The members of the Movement have joined and supported them in making sure that they were not abandoned and in getting the authorities to take them into account.

Widespread consultation and diverse exchanges led our members to collectively decide our 2013–17 *Common Ambitions*. Above, a snapshot from one of the written presentions. Members also make use of audio-visual presentations in several languages.

International Leadership Team, and ATD members with regional or international responsibilities, a draft of the *Common Ambitions* for 2013–17 resulted, with content as follows:

• Central Focus: Reaching out to those whose contribution is missing;

• Priority 1: Building knowledge and accessing education — every mind counts;

• Priority 2: Shaping a people-centered and earth-friendly economic vision;

• Priority 3: Communicating for human rights and peace.

These *Common Ambitions* can be found in an Appendix at the end of this book.

Additional dialogues then took place with members of ATD Fourth World at the local level to confirm agreement about these ambitions and about the language used to address them. During this process, people were consulted individually by email, telephone, or home visits for those without access to other means of communication. These consultations included non-directive interviews on a given theme and requests for reactions to the draft *Common Ambitions*.

Publicizing our *Common Ambitions*: Written and audio-visual presentations of these ambitions were released in English, French, and Spanish on the World Day for Overcoming Poverty. The videos, which show projects in a wide variety of cultural contexts, have been made available on our website in order to make the *Common Ambitions* accessible to people of different backgrounds. They are a tool for all our local groups and teams, as well as for existing and potential partners.

The participation of all: An ethical approach to evaluation and planning

People who have experienced extreme poverty and social exclusion say that ATD Fourth World is a place where they feel that their presence, their voices, and their participation are not only appreciated but also sought out. We make a point of coming together for festive occasions as well as for meetings and for mutual support during hard times. Whatever the situation, all our members look for ways to reach out to others and to cultivate a sense of community among people of different backgrounds. Far from being "beneficiaries," people in poverty drive ATD Fourth World forward.

That said, it requires great effort for people living in poverty to participate in evaluation and planning. The obstacles are clear. Not everyone will be able to attend a meeting, especially not those whose lives are the hardest. Among those who do attend, the risk is great that some participants may not speak their minds, but only react to what others say. In order to train our local groups to assess and plan their work with all members, approaches adapted to the local context must be proposed. For example, our group on Reunion Island began by making home visits to conduct open-ended interviews starting with a few simple questions:

- What does ATD Fourth World mean to you?

- What do you get out of it? What do people you know who live in poverty get out of it?

- Who are the people/families/young people that you think ATD Fourth World should reach out to? How do you think this should be done? For what kind of project?

- What kind of new project do you think ATD Fourth World should start? How do you think current projects should be done differently?

After these interviews, it was easier for people in poverty to attend a meeting with others to talk over the questions. Ideas that emerged from the interviews were read aloud and written on a blackboard. Links between these ideas were analyzed. Which ones were similar? Which ones were unique? Going around the table ensured that everyone was able to contribute ideas, without the floor being monopolized by those who were most comfortable speaking up. This approach drew out thoughts about discrimination, racism, and social exclusion. Participants also discussed what can make it possible for people from different religions, economic backgrounds, and ethnicities to get to know one another. The participants expressed their pride in this meaningful way of working together. They agreed on two observations:

"With ATD Fourth World, we learn to speak out."

"We hesitate to talk to our children's teachers or other parents from their school."

These contrasting observations highlighted the need to work on how each person can make the transition from speaking in a place where she or he is comfortable to speaking in more formal and less familiar settings.

At the meetings held to analyze the ideas that emerged from the interviews, the group drew up a list of issues, and then each person was asked which issues he or she found the most important and why. Finally, the group as a whole chose a single issue to focus on. Following these meetings, a paper drafted to share this issue with others was discussed in phone calls and home visits in order to finalize the language. The same steps were taken as the group became part of the worldwide long-distance exchanges and entered into dialogue with groups on other continents,

On Reunion Island (in the Indian Ocean), members of ATD enjoy a Family Day event in 2014 while discussing education, one of the priorities chosen during our evaluation and planning process.

each one working to understand the differences between their local contexts. Consulting one another to choose one important issue proved to be a powerful tool for developing a common understanding among diverse people who have come together to fight poverty.

Once a group has conducted an evaluation with the broad participation of its members, the process becomes easier to replicate. People who participate in this approach can explain it to newcomers, and many of them gain self-assurance and acquire new skills with which to take on responsibility in their communities. The more our members — including those who live in poverty — participate fully in the evaluation and planning process, the more enthusiasm and confidence they have for joining a project or for collaborating with others to run it.

Ms. Maritza Orozco. "Being able to share has created strength within us. We have to prepare people to break the silence."

Maritza Orozco, a mother in a low-income family in Guatemala, described the changes that took place for her. Speaking about her role in the participatory action-research project, "Extreme Poverty Is Violence — Breaking the Silence — Searching for Peace," she said:

Something new has arisen in me. Being able to share with [other] families created strength within us. I always did want to support and help others, that's how I am, but I didn't have knowledge. I learned that we have to defend our rights. We have to say, "Yes we can, yes we know." I felt stronger. The motivation was born in me to visit families that I hadn't visited before. This came together with the wish to share more. The way we worked together was good because each of us could speak about our own experience. I think we should continue to seek out and visit new families, and to be always united to go and reach out to those who are still missing. I think there are more people who could work on something like this. We have to prepare people to break the silence. Preparing them means continuing to visit and share with them.

Having been part of the collective effort to break the silence about the violence of poverty, Ms. Orozco feels more capable of reaching out to others whose contribution is "still missing" because of the ways poverty may isolate them. Many of those who contributed to our international evaluation and planning stressed what a waste it is that society is deprived of the experience and knowledge of people who live their lives in resistance to extreme poverty. ATD Fourth World has always sought out people whose poverty has prevented them from gaining the confidence and skills needed to participate. These participants show all of us how much we need their contribution and that of others like them. This is why Ms. Orozco's words — "to reach out to those who are still missing" — are the central focus of our *Common Ambitions* for 2013–17.

6

Sustaining Our Collective Will
to Continue Moving Forward

Recognizing and defending the rights of people living in poverty is a demanding endeavor. It requires continually seeking out people at risk of being left out, because every person matters. It requires creating and sustaining a partnership where each person is able to develop her or his voice in order to participate freely. To meet these challenges, we must strive to sustain the collective will that all of us need in order to move forward together.

The unrelenting harshness of extreme poverty can be a permanent source of despair: when we can't afford to put a meal on the table, when we are evicted, when social services remove custody of our children. For people who were born into these constant crises, as for people who choose to join them in solidarity, it is inevitable that there are times when the courage to move forward is lacking. An activist from the Ivory Coast says that when he can't even afford to provide for his family, he questions his manhood. At the same time, he adds, "I am a man because I am capable of love, and I choose to love. The one battle worth fighting is solidarity with those who are the most tired. If you have love, you are a man of peace." An activist from Switzerland who carries

In the Ivory Coast, ATD Fourth World first began in a penal camp where prisoners formed a "Club of Knowledge." This logo they designed conveys the creativity and values they nurtured.

Working with clay: this and other artistic workshops were part of
an international event during our 2012 General Assembly process.
Each participant created objects to share the story of the gathering
with other members who were not able to be present.

an overall responsibility for our work in her country says, "Our steps are
small ones, and we must never forget to turn back to see who has not
dared take the first step. We must return for that person. That's my daily
life, I have to do it every day — but sometimes we stop to rest because
there are times when we just can't walk one more step."

Over time, the need to rely on one another creates strong bonds
among our members, fostering a solidarity that genuinely supports each
of us, through our own development, to offer the best of ourselves in the
effort to make a world where all people can offer the best of themselves.
Nevertheless, choosing again, day after day, to turn back for others to
make sure we move forward together is a challenge. All of us — activists,
volunteers, and allies[62] — plan regular times for encouraging one another,
renewing our courage, and developing ways to sustain our collective will
to move forward together. This takes place internationally through occa-

---

62. Fourth World allies are people of all walks of life acting in solidarity with people who
live in extreme poverty.

sional General Assembly processes for all senior members. It also takes place locally and nationally on a regular basis. In speaking about what sustains her will to be involved, one member, Jean Stallings of the United States, spoke about love and respect:

As a child, I didn't feel I was loved. One day when a Sunday school teacher told me she loved me, I started to feel I deserved to be loved. That's what I want for others: that they have a chance to meet people who will tell them they are worthy of being loved. When we say we accept someone the way they are, that doesn't mean that we don't believe they can change their life. It means we respect someone as they are, we respect what they are going through. And that can

Ms. Jean Stallings.

be a starting point for changing things together. It means believing that the person we meet is already resisting poverty somehow, maybe just by protecting themselves or trying to share something. We can recognize that in each person and then leave them free to choose the next step. That's what's enduring in our way of being present to people in ATD Fourth World. Not everyone is ready to join in a meeting or a project, but with those who aren't, we can meet them where they are, accept and respect them, and believe that they will look for the next step.

Renewing our courage can also entail choosing freely, once again, a commitment that may seem incomprehensible to colleagues. Sandrine Dandjinou is an ally who works at a university in Burkina Faso. She says, "When I tell my colleagues that I have made a commitment to working with children living in the streets, they say I'm sticking my nose where it doesn't belong. They say I'm not normal. But just what is normal? Is it normal not to be concerned for others?" Sandrine can sustain her will to continue this dialogue with her colleagues because of the times we take collectively to deepen and reflect on this commitment.

Ms. Sandrine Dandjinou (at right) with fellow participants
Ms. Hélène Giacobino (at left) and Ms. Florence Kandolo at our
March 2013 participatory evaluation seminar in Burkina Faso.

During one of these meetings, several of our members in Southeast
Asia communicated their feelings and thoughts. In one exercise, participants presented an image of something that they thought represented
ATD Fourth World. Several people chose photos of coconut trees, which
many cultures consider the tree of life. Vanessa Joos, a Belgian volunteer
based in the Philippines, was one of them. She said of her choice:

"As volunteers with ATD, we need to stay well rooted in the daily
life of many different people — walking, working, writing, fighting,
and dreaming together. It's not always easy, it moves us in many
ways, and sometimes we get tired, and are leaning a lot to one side
or another, like a coconut tree bending over near the seashore. [...]
Almost all parts of the coconut tree are useful: just like, for me, ATD
and being a volunteer striving with others to end poverty touches
our life in all its aspects. And we try to reach out to all members of
society, with all means. After a while we can bear some fruit; the
fruit will fall in the water or in the sand nearby or it may float away,
sometimes very far to start something new (or the same?)"

Ms. Vanessa Joos (front, left) with ATD members in the Philippines.

The connections among all of us also renew our courage. In 2012, one of our members from the Ivory Coast traveled to France as part of our General Assembly process. He carried with him an album of photos and correspondence tracing the history of our movement in the Ivory Coast over decades and its many links with our members around the world. Some of the photos were taken in a penal camp where he had been incarcerated in Bouaké, and where one of our volunteers had hosted a "Club of Knowledge" with him and other prisoners. After this man's release, when rebels ransacked that penal camp during the first Ivorian civil war, he undertook a dangerous journey back to the camp in order to save the album.

Safegarding history and links: This album, offered to the Joseph Wresinski Center in France, traces the decades-long history of ATD Fourth World in the Ivory Coast.

121

He says, "The rebels were ignorant of our history together, they would have destroyed everything." This is why in 2012 he brought the album he treasured to France, where he entrusted it to the International Joseph Wresinski Center. In this center, the history that the album recounts of building mutual respect and solidarity among people and peoples inspires and encourages those who see it.

It is important to us to build these links between different countries, because the stigmatization and exclusion that accompany extreme poverty often require new links in order to break the pattern. Time and again, people enduring inhuman treatment say, "This is how our parents and grandparents lived too; it's our fate." Within low-income communities in every country, there can be dynamic leaders who refuse to consider thinking together with the most marginalized people. The reasons vary: "They will spread illness," or "They have nothing to contribute," or simply, "They will slow us down." But the refusal is clear. If people who are used to being treated this way are to change the way they see themselves, they must meet people who have undergone similar treatment in a completely different context. The same is true of community leaders. Breaking a pattern of local exclusion can become possible when leaders are able to

Honduras: Mr. Noé Cabrera, here visiting Doña Guadalupe, recognizes the efforts of families struggling to overcome poverty.

work with others elsewhere who are ready to do the same. This is why we regularly organize meetings among people living in extreme poverty in different countries, and also why volunteers are often invited to join teams outside their own country, both to learn from the people they will meet and to help people who have been excluded to see themselves in a new light. Little by little, these links continue to grow, connecting us from person to person and place to place, and fostering new relationships. We oppose the practice of some countries sending "experts" to instruct other countries, given that no nation has known how to eradicate poverty or to govern in a way that allows for pooling everyone's intelligence, courage, and commitments. Instead, we are developing a new form of international cooperation, where people of every country can both learn from and teach one another across borders.

As we build this solidarity among nations and among people, we have to find ways of renewing our courage in the face of despair. Noé Cabrera, an activist in Honduras, does this by recognizing people like Doña Daniella who, after her daughter's disappearance, went for a month without speaking, keeping her head down so no one in the neighborhood would approach her, and unable to share her pain with another soul. When she was able to speak again with another of our members, she said, "This is the only place I can talk." Noé adds, "Today, society does not yet recognize all the efforts and courage of these families, but here today, we recognize them."

Conclusion

_____

"All human beings are born free and equal in dignity and rights."
— The Universal Declaration of Human Rights

Around the world, women, men, and young people living in poverty strive to live in dignity and dedicate their efforts to the future of children. For all those around them, they search for peace rooted in respect for human rights. In the past year, some of these people have lost their lives to the violence of poverty, which continues to strike down children and parents without mercy. All of us who survive carry deep within us the aspiration: never again.

- Never again should a newborn be at high risk of ill health with no access to health care;

- Never again should children, from their first day at school, be treated as less worthy of respect than others, and be told that they are doomed to failure;

- Never again should anyone be abused or degraded by an employer;

- Never again should indignities and humiliations be heaped upon homeless families reduced to scavenging to survive, their children taken from them by the violence of street life or by social services, and their health ravaged by poverty;

- Never again should anyone's safety be jeopardized by being repeatedly evicted and having to raise a family in places where no one would choose to live.

In 2009–12, when members of ATD Fourth World broke the silence about the hidden violence of extreme poverty, important steps forward were taken. The first was to challenge the image of "the violent poor" that traps society into criminalizing poverty and worsening its effects. Challenging this image opened doors for people in poverty, who developed

Families like Mr. Rolando's, shown here under the bridge where they lived for years in the Tulay community of Manila, strive to reestablish livelihoods and community solidarity in resettlement sites far outside the city.

a collective awareness of the need to break the silence and to cultivate mutual understanding as a path toward peace. This work also increased the capital of trust between people living in poverty and others. This capital of trust can give more security than gates and walls; it can provide safety through new ways of meeting, getting to know, supporting, and recognizing one another.

At the same time, this work on the violence of poverty made it possible to reveal some of the many hidden ways in which people in extreme poverty have long been searching for peace:

- When families are displaced, they are often welcomed by families whose own living conditions are the most fragile, as has happened in Lebanon. People like Abir Rizk, despite feeling torn between anger and peace, do as much as they can to "open our hearts" to everyone.

- In the resettlement project in the Philippines, even as families struggle with the loss of their livelihoods, many of them continue to invest efforts in building solidarity with their neighbors. They may take the initiative to go repeatedly around the community and

ask how the others are doing.
Some of them help to identify
families who need support
in understanding the process
or in fulfilling the necessary
requirements.

- During the human rights
consultations, Pagakaew
Nuian and others took the risk
of speaking out about the fear
of the police and of landlords
that many others endure
in silence, condemned to
stigmatization and inhuman
living conditions.

Ms. Pagakaew Nuian speaks
about human rights as a Thai
delegate to the October 17, 2007,
commemoration on the Trocadero
Human Rights Plaza in Paris.

- People like Véréna Caffin
find ways to defy a public discourse that pits people of different
backgrounds against one another in low-income housing projects
and emergency shelters. By bearing witness to the greatness of
her friend's life, even as his body was left in a parking lot before
being buried in an unidentified grave, she nourished the sense of
community that can end exclusion.

- People living in poverty have long known that social change will
come not from accusations but from developing ways for everyone
to get to know and understand better the realities of their different
situations. This is why we undertook an evaluation of the impact
of the Millennium Development Goals (MDGs) as an opportunity
for people in poverty to contribute their intelligence to shaping
sustainable development so that no one will be left behind.

Looking back, we are proud that a new approach to solidarity and
to thinking and acting together made possible this collaborative MDG
evaluation done by two thousand people — most living in poverty, others
women and men who fight poverty either as individuals or from within
public or private institutions. A similar collaboration among our members
led us to formulate the four *Common Ambitions* that will shape our goals

(Above and below) Peer study groups in the Philippines helped shape our participatory evaluation of the MDGs, *Challenge 2015: Towards Sustainable Development that Leaves No One Behind.*

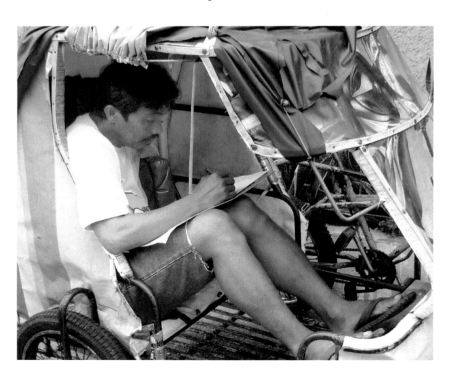

In Peru with UN expert Mr. José Bengoa (back row, wearing glasses)
at the close of a 2007 consultation seminar on the
Guiding Principles on Extreme Poverty and Human Rights.

for the next four years. In France, where the tone denigrating and stigmatizing people who depend on welfare has become increasingly harsh, the work to challenge discrimination based on poverty is nevertheless moving forward. We believe that if French law is broadened to include poverty-based discrimination, it will become a tool to help build more harmonious relationships, both among the diverse populations in low-income housing projects and within the whole of French society.

People living in extreme poverty express a twofold concern: being able to live without violence; and being able to live in communities where everyone is linked to one another in concord and goodwill. These concerns are interdependent. As international institutions and governments work toward post-2015 sustainable development goals, it is crucial to understand that a truly sustainable world is one in which no one is left behind or discriminated against. If we are to live sustainably on our troubled planet, now and on behalf of generations to come, we must create forums that constitute opportunities for long-term dialogue between people living in extreme poverty and the rest of society. These forums where we discuss experiences, knowledge, and new approaches to working together enable us to offer new answers for the challenges of our times.

These are the questions our members address when those in Peru reveal their personal hardships in order to shape international human rights guidelines; when those in France study Quebec's discrimination laws and try to create precedents for others; and when people in dozens of countries collaborate to find new ways to reach out to people isolated by extreme poverty and to work toward peace together. Even before World War II ended, world leaders and visionaries met to imagine how nations would be able to unite to build a post-war future. Today, it is people living in extreme poverty, and subjected to exclusion and discrimination, who meet to imagine a different future. At the very heart of armed conflict, of environmental catastrophes, of economic crises that endanger nations, and of rural and urban zones that have become unlivable, they are moving forward with determination to shape a world of "freedom from want and freedom from fear." Recognizing these efforts would be a decisive step toward transforming national and international institutions so that one day all artisans of peace can contribute their unique experience, skills, and intelligence as we strive to shape a world where every person, every family, and every community can live in peace.

ATD Fourth World's
Common Ambitions for 2013–17

Central Focus: Reaching Out to Those Whose Contribution Is Missing

The violence of extreme poverty locks people and families into a terrible spiral of ignorance, deprivation, contempt and silence. Despite this, they resist day by day by surviving, by joining others, and by building a sense of community. Their resistance gives them a unique experience and knowledge that society overlooks or ignores. In so doing, society robs itself of a contribution that is irreplaceable for facing today's global challenges. These people and families are missing from all the places where society takes shape.

As members of ATD Fourth World, we join people and families who are abandoned and stigmatized because of extreme poverty. Standing all together in dignity means acting in ways that allow all people to be taken into account and counted on wherever decisions are made that affect humanity. It means creating an opportunity for the world: when no one is left behind, projects and policies can bring people together instead of dividing them; we can stem the tide of inequality; and we can draw closer to the ideals of justice, freedom, and peace.

This central focus is a compass for everything we undertake, both on our own and with partners, and wherever else each of us may be involved, whether in our communities, places of worship, political parties, labor unions, and so on. This focus is the key criterion for evaluating our *Common Ambitions* for 2013–17.

Working toward this central focus involves all of us — activists, allies, and volunteers — and particularly the members of the Volunteer Corps, who have a responsibility for supporting all those who take risks in implementing this approach. No one reaching out to the most vulnerable should be alone with this challenge, and all of our teams should be creative in this endeavor.

Three questions can guide us:

- Does our team or group work together and support one another to "go and seek out those who are still missing"?

- Even when we lack the capacity for our projects to include a greater number of people, do we find ways to welcome new participants who are recognized by other participants as being in situations of great difficulty? What initiatives do we take and what means do we mobilize for this purpose?

- Do our projects enable the expression and contribution of these people? Does their presence and participation contribute to identifiable changes for themselves, for us, for their community, and for everyone?

What practices does "reaching the most vulnerable people" imply within ATD Fourth World?

- Addressing the question in each of our teams or groups of **how to reach people** who are the most socially isolated by extreme poverty.

- Supporting one another to reach **those whose rights are denied** or made subject to conditions, **those who are socially stigmatized** and discriminated against, and **those who are subjected to violence**, whether they belong to the local population, or are immigrants or displaced people, living in rural or urban settings.

- Relying on the **strengths of communities** that make efforts for everyone to have a place.

- Evaluating and regularly revisiting our choices so that our presence and action remain open to **those who are still hidden** or marginalized or who have difficulties participating in what we undertake.

- Recognizing and supporting the involvement of those who, in spite of their own daily struggle against poverty, **remain in solidarity with the most disadvantaged people**. Their determination to show solidarity, sometimes beyond their means, is often misunderstood or considered irresponsible by society at large.

- Providing opportunities both to get to know each other and to find the signs and actions that foster mutual recognition and respect for everyone's dignity. Beyond our teams and across borders, **sharing experiences and ideas** for reaching the most vulnerable.

- Enabling people with an experience of extreme poverty to **participate in writing the story of their families, neighborhoods, or communities.** In writing this collective history of people in poverty and reclaiming their forgotten role, they contribute to recording humanity's common history in ways that deny no person, no social class, no nation, and thereby prepare peace.

What practices does "reaching the most vulnerable people" imply in our links with others who are not members of ATD Fourth World?

- Connecting with people or **groups who are also reaching out** to people in extreme poverty in order to learn from them.

- Raising awareness that the experience, **vision, and questions of those living in extreme poverty** are relevant for guiding development that is truly sustainable.

- Fostering the participation of **people with an experience of extreme poverty**, in reciprocity with other stakeholders, in elaborating knowledge in all fields.

- Continuing to seek out **high-level events and dialogues** as part of our efforts to enable people living in extreme poverty to be heard by national, regional, and world leaders.

Three Priorities

1. *Building knowledge and accessing education — every mind counts*
2. *Shaping a people-centered and earth-friendly economic vision*
3. *Communicating for human rights and peace*

1. Building Knowledge and Accessing Education — Every Mind Counts

Why?

Prevented from benefiting from the common store of knowledge, people in extreme poverty struggle continually for access to it for themselves and their children. Education for all people at all ages[63] — through schools, access to culture, and ongoing learning of all kinds — must be a priority for all of society because it is far from being achieved. Because people in situations of extreme poverty are prevented from expressing their own experience, they cannot contribute to projects that affect them. Knowledge from the life experience of people in poverty is an untapped resource that is indispensable for developing the emancipatory knowledge needed to understand the world and to improve life for all.[64] Wasting the intelligence of women, men, young people, and children living in poverty is a serious form of discrimination.

The emergence of a knowledge economy and new media opens the door to initiatives that will pool the intelligence of all people. These initiatives should draw on the potential of ever-developing communication networks, and renew the production of knowledge and the ways in which it is taught and acquired through partnership and cooperation among all stakeholders.

Education for all becomes possible when all concerned — parents, children, and young people, communities, schools, and other learning centers — give one another recognition and interact in constructive and complementary ways.

---

63. The Education for All movement, led by UNESCO, is a global commitment to provide quality basic education for all children, young people, and adults.

64. This was demonstrated in a participatory research project on Merging Knowledge between academia and Fourth World People's Universities in which people with a personal experience of poverty were actors in creating knowledge. Cf. Fourth World–University Research Group. The Merging of Knowledge: People in Poverty and Academics Thinking Together. University Press of America, 2007. Also see, Defraigne-Tardieu, Geneviève. *L'université populaire Quart Monde. La construction du savoir émancipatoire.* Presses universitaires de Paris Ouest, 2012.

In several countries, this ambition has already guided our pilot projects and partnerships with others. In Tanzania, members wrote "Going to School." Members in the United States created a CD-ROM called Unleashing Hidden Potential. In France, Workshops for School led to a national conference. And for our evaluation of the Millennium Development Goals, parents, children, and educators contributed to knowledge work on education in Bolivia, Burkina Faso, Guatemala, Haiti, Madagascar, Mauritius, Peru, and the Philippines. Based on all this work, we addressed specific policy proposals to national and international policy makers.[65]

Main areas to work on

Our long history of knowledge-sharing projects — Tapori, Street Libraries, Festivals of Learning, Story Gardens, etc. — and these recent pilot projects lead us today to the following priorities:

A. Discovering together what knowledge is useful to understand the world and take charge of one's own life.

- Identifying and recognizing existing life skills (passed on by families, communities, and cultures) and their complementarity with the knowledge taught in schools or training institutions. These life skills may have been learned through cultural traditions, from work experience, from knowing how to live together with others, or from a sense of solidarity.

- Exploring and experimenting within our knowledge-sharing projects, and in schools or training centers, how **combining life skills with academic or technical knowledge** can help young people and children to grow within their families and communities and prepare them to be citizens of the world.

- Stimulating the joy of learning together, **unleashing hidden potential** and creativity to bolster confidence that everyone can learn. Giving extra support to young people involved in

---

65. ATD Fourth World. *Challenge 2015: Towards Sustainable Development that Leaves No One Behind*, June 2014, pages 15–16 and 23–24.

disadvantaged neighborhoods to share knowledge through books, art, music, etc.

- Intensifying **our contribution to education** and ongoing learning for all, based on partnership and cooperation

B. Supporting families as the first place of education.

- Learning to notice and support efforts and **initiatives that parents take** for their children's future. Raising awareness that parents are the first partners for their children's academic success makes it possible for teachers and children's extended families to act in a spirit of cooperation and complementarity.

- Identifying and addressing **barriers to schooling**, such as: hidden or secondary costs for supposedly free education; discrimination and stigmatization in places of learning that increase children's fear of failure and prevent parents from communicating with the world of education. Making Tapori[66] better known as a key tool for ending bullying.

- Developing partnerships with institutions, training centers, and alternative or informal education programs that are committed to realizing **the right to education for all.**

- Promoting **cooperation among learners** and being creative in addressing the fact that competition can undermine the school experience for both its "winners" and its "losers," as noted by teachers during the project "Together, Building a School Where Everyone Succeeds,"[67] and by young people and adults living in poverty in the evaluation of the Millennium Development Goals, in particular with regard to a project where the pedagogy of non-abandonment was shown to enrich education for all.[68]

---

66. Tapori is a movement of children from different background and from around the world. Wherever they live, Tapori children stand up for others so that all children will have the same chances.

67. This French project is documented in a book by Régis Félix and eleven teachers, all members of ATD Fourth World. *Tous peuvent réussir ! Partir des élèves dont on n'attend rien.* Published in 2013 by Editions Quart Monde and Chronique Sociale.

68. This project, which took place in Madagascar in 2006–11, is outlined in the videoclip, "Agents of Change: New Technologies for All."

Making known **the Merging Knowledge approach** as one that fosters a relationship between families resisting extreme poverty and all the other actors in their children's education.

C. Developing our ongoing learning programs to prepare ourselves for an ambitious implementation of these commitments. Making available to people and families we meet the means and the most effective tools for sharing knowledge.

2. Shaping a People-Centered and Earth-Friendly Economic Vision

Why?

Today's dominant economic system creates a permanent state of crisis for people in extreme poverty who are subject to extreme exploitation and constrained to uselessness. Insecure jobs, harmful and humiliating working conditions, chronic unemployment, and rising food costs — all cause despair. Unscrupulous employers, who require their workers to forfeit pay or to steal from a competitor, pervert the hope of decent work into a cycle of dependency. Yet, day after day, people in extreme poverty struggle and toil to provide for their families. With limited means, they organize themselves to adapt to the often extremely polluted environment in which they are forced to live. To get by, they invent their own informal work and networks of solidarity. Contrary to the widely-held belief that they are a burden, their activity in fact contributes to the global economy and to the common good. It is part of a multifaceted economy where alongside formal work in the public or private sectors is domestic labor — largely ignored by statistics — and the informal work sector that makes up an increasingly large part of the global labor market.[69]

---

69. "The concept of informal employment refers to jobs or activities of production and sale of goods or services which are legal but not regulated or protected by the state. On average in the world, more than half of the jobs in the non-agricultural sector can be considered informal. In some regions, such as sub-Saharan Africa and South Asia, the figure is at least 80 percent. The persistence of this phenomenon prevents employment from having a positive impact on poverty reduction." Jütting, J and De Laiglesia, J.R. *Is Informal Normal? Towards More and Better Jobs in Developing Countries*, OECD Development Center, 2009, page 11.

Many people around the world, individually or in networks, are engaged in important explorations of alternative economic models whose aim is not profit or accumulating capital, but fostering the well-being of people and communities, especially the most disadvantaged ones. These efforts to develop a social economy or a sharing economy include micro-credit, fair trade, cooperatives, mutual organizations, and social enterprises. Other projects change people's daily life with no exchange of money, for instance through voluntary efforts to build homes or prevent flooding, and through networks where people trade services or share their know-how.

In continuity with our experience over several generations — and during our 2008–12 Contract of Common Commitments — working on programs to provide access to professional training and work for populations in extreme poverty,[70] today we are choosing as one of our ambitions to work together with people living in poverty in order to promote an economy that benefits all people.

By speaking of a people-centered and earth-friendly economic vision, we mean:

- an economy that respects the human rights of all people and communities, and the dignity of each person and their community values and practices; and that preserves the rights and opportunities of future generations.

- an economy that does not waste people's intelligence and know-how, and that does not plunder the planet's resources or harm biodiversity.

- an economy that encourages sharing, solidarity, and the cooperation that strengthens social ties and develops the sense of a common good.

---

70. Cf. Godinot, Xavier. *On voudrait connaître le secret du travail*, Editions de l'Atelier/ Fourth World Editions, 1995. Report on international Working and Learning Together Seminar, ATD Fourth World, June 2010. *L'entreprise réinventée: Travailler et Apprendre Ensemble, Editions de l'Atelier/Fourth* World Editions, 2012. See also the video New Technologies for All about a project in Madagascar in 2006–11.

Main areas to work on

The projects we develop will vary across the different economic and cultural contexts in which we find ourselves.

In the framework of building understanding, of monitoring projects, and of dialogue within ATD Fourth World:

- By doing projects together and living as neighbors, deepening our **knowledge of the efforts made by people in extreme poverty** to make ends meet, to influence their environment, and to connect with their community.

- Continuing "Working and Learning Together" projects as part of an international network where access to decent work or to various income-generating activities is linked to community building and to the goals of full employment, decent work, and social protection for all.

- Exploring and experimenting with **initiatives for the public good** (access to water, protection of the environment, improvement of housing, etc.) or for fair trade; and promoting community resilience and self-provisioning of food and other goods.

- Participating in dialogues (with universities, think tanks, business leaders, etc.) about **the economy and its regulation**, both nationally and internationally.

- Developing our partnerships with labor unions and all stakeholders to **obtain full employment and decent work for all**, and to implement social protection floors in every country in reference to human rights obligations and the recommendations of the International Labour Organization.[71]

- Participating in networks aiming to **humanize the economy**, and in alternative networks that contribute to shaping an economy for the well-being of all.

---

71. Advocating for an international mechanism to fund and support their implementation wherever available resources are too limited.

Our experience has taught us that in this field, determination should be paired with caution:

- Providing money or economic opportunity can trigger jealousies that divide communities instead of strengthening solidarity. Together with the people whose poverty makes them most vulnerable to these divisions, we must create conditions suitable for them to take part in the projects.

- Economic projects may require long-term financial and human investments. Failing to plan clearly for this may put a team at risk of losing the trust of the most disadvantaged people.

- Divergent and controversial views on finance and the corporate world can divide even the most generous and committed people, including some among ATD Fourth World's most active members.

3. Communicating for Human Rights and Peace

Why?

Our work on violence, extreme poverty, and peace, and our evaluation of the impact of the Millennium Development Goals renewed our understanding of extreme poverty. They sharpened our ability to speak of the unbearable injustice of extreme poverty and showed how people enduring these conditions, and those working alongside them, have made a commitment to working for peace.

Ending extreme poverty depends on public organizing, advocacy, and civic engagement in society. Everyone's efforts are needed, and it is important that everyone have opportunities to show their solidarity in the struggle to respect human rights. By encouraging civic engagement, we can also have greater freedom for working toward social justice by expanding our network of friends and donors to broaden our grassroots funding base.

We are in a world of accelerating communication. While this has pitfalls that can sometimes intensify prejudice or create a whirlpool of false perceptions, there are also a growing number of ways for people worldwide to be in touch, to influence one another, and to create positive social change together. We want all our members to be able to take advantage of the possibilities offered by modern means of communication, while remaining linked to those without access to them, and while continuing to stress the importance of people meeting face to face.

Main areas to work on

Engaging and communicating.

- **Integrating communication** into the work of all our teams and collaborating to pool expertise in communicating, organizing, and advocacy.

- Exploring techniques to encourage civic engagement by **using the strength of social networks** and other modern means of communication, learning from the experience of young people. Strategizing together about access to, use of, and possibilities of these tools.

Encouraging civic involvement and stimulating dialogue

- Learning about and **supporting the involvement of other people or organizations** who are close to people in extreme poverty, who take steps so that no one is left behind in their neighborhood or in their children's school. They are looking for new ways to build a sense of community, one that respects each person and the environment. With these people, we strengthen the movement for overcoming poverty, particularly through Tapori, the Forum on Overcoming Extreme Poverty, and events for the World Day for Overcoming Poverty.

- Running public communications campaigns and **inviting more people to stay in touch with us** through a regular practice of organizing campaigns and "friend-raising."

- Highlighting the meaning and importance of the different **ways that allies make a long-term commitment to ATD Fourth World**. Inviting the general public to act in solidarity with people in

extreme poverty by sharing creative approaches that have been
developed by our individual members around the world as part of
appeals for civic engagement.

- Making known **the life, the work, and the writings of Fr. Joseph
  Wresinski**, founder of ATD Fourth World. The power of his
  call to action remains more relevant than ever as we prepare for
  2017, which will mark the centennial of his birth as well as thirty
  years since the appeal he launched on October 17, 1987. These
  anniversaries will be a special opportunity for local, national, and
  international public events, and for making social change.

- Developing our **capacity for dialogue** with stakeholders in
  different fields that influence the world: the economic, public
  policy, and philosophical and religious underpinnings on which
  societies are built; and movements for social and environmental
  justice.

- Making known the **Guiding Principles on Extreme Poverty
  and Human Rights** as a reference for policy proposals, together
  with the implementation handbook that was prepared by a
  group of non-governmental organizations[72] to help make these
  guidelines known to community-level workers, policy makers,
  and practitioners.

Making time for ongoing learning and sustaining
our will to continue choosing to fight poverty.

- Making sure that no one is alone and that **everyone has the chance
  to talk** about key issues coming from his or her involvement in
  ATD Fourth World, whether these issues are linked to a project,

---

72. Available for download at: http://atd-fourthworld.org/wp-content/uploads/sites
/5/2015/05/2015-09-01-GuidingPrinplsEPHR-HANDBOOK-EN-ATD_FI_Handbook
_English_WEB-1.pdf. The handbook was created by: Arab Network for Development,
BICE (International Catholic Child Bureau), Center for Economic and Social Rights,
FIAN, International Commission of Jurists, International Council of Women, International Disability Alliance, International Federation of Social Workers, Legal
Resource Centre of South Africa, PLAN International, and the World YWCA. This
project was initiated and coordinated by ATD Fourth World and Franciscans Inter-
national.

to relations with others from a person's own background or community, to the search for meaning, or to a person's beliefs.[73]

- The International Leadership Team will initiate a reflection on new ways that we can support all our members, sustain our commonality of purpose, and take on responsibilities together.

---

73. During our evaluation, a member in the Central African Republic said, "We are awed by the strength of our young people for overcoming their own difficulties to continue their involvement in their neighborhoods. […] This commitment [to children] gives even more meaning to their lives. […] Supporting them is our moral duty."

About Volumes 1 and 3

Y̶ou may also be interested in the following volumes of *Artisans of Peace Overcoming Poverty.*

VOLUME 1
A People-Centered Movement

- **A chapter on the origins of ATD Fourth World** retraces why and how Joseph Wresinski launched this movement in 1957.

- **Thirty years in Haiti** shares the story of people, beginning in 1984, who looked for ways to cope with fear in their "no-go" district by trying to "become examples for the neighborhood so there would be peace." The World Day for Overcoming Poverty also became a touchstone for these efforts. Following the 2010 earthquake, our members climbed to the furthest reaches of this district to ensure that no one would be forgotten, and joined in a UN call for "Unheard voices thinking about Haiti's tomorrow."

- **People choosing to work toward peace** come from all backgrounds: activists, born into poverty and taking responsibility in their own communities; allies, who use the fact that they are accepted to challenge colleagues or neighbors to act differently toward people in poverty; and the Fourth World Volunteer Corps, which shares a collective responsibility for no one to be left behind. No one is too young to make a difference, from young people in France and Senegal, to children in the Democratic Republic of the Congo. Through a Forum on Overcoming Extreme Poverty, individuals and non-profits who are not members of ATD Fourth World can also share ideas and encouragement with one another.

- **Inventing ways to live in peace together.** Because poverty can isolate people behind stereotypes and reduce them to silence, participation in Fourth World People's Universities is a key way

145

to begin thinking together. A Merging Knowledge approach can make it possible for people of all backgrounds to develop new knowledge, drawing on the hidden intelligence of people in poverty. Concerning training and employment, both the pedagogy of non-abandonment and projects where professionals agree to share risks with the long-term unemployed make possible a new approach to decent work and to excellence. Finally, beyond thinking and working together, the act of creation can help to overcome poverty because it transforms the way people see themselves and one another. Street Libraries and Story Gardens are ways to share the means for creative expression, culture, art, and beauty. This chapter concludes with a personal essay about creativity and culture, called "Dreaming Permit."

VOLUME 3

Understanding the Violence of Poverty

- **Diversity and exclusion in France and Belgium — building a sense of belonging.** Despite terrorist attacks that have thrown into stark relief the challenges of unifying society without leaving anyone behind, residents of low-income districts take part in our People's University sessions to risk starting dialogues that can open doors and enable people to overcome a sense of despair.

- **Understanding and reclaiming the past in the Philippines, Switzerland, and the United States.** History was written by the powerful, leaving mostly unwritten the stories of countless people forced into exile or homelessness. In the Philippines and in the United States, recording and understanding the courage and hopes of homeless families enable us to reclaim our collective history. In Switzerland, the experience of families in poverty who were subjected to unilateral decisions that removed their children from their care prompted the government in 2013 to revisit its own past and acknowledge its responsibility.

- **Resistance to stigmatization in the United Kingdom — the Roles We Play.** A public campaign against welfare fraud distorts the truth and reinforces vitriolic stereotypes about people in poverty. In an effort to resist this, our members decided to make known their faces and personal stories through a book and an interactive exhibit/workshop called "The Roles We Play: Recognising the Contributions of People in Poverty."

- **The violence of poverty and the search for peace.** People living in poverty are feared as a source of violence, banished from public spaces, and kept at bay by gated communities. Few other people see their efforts to reach out to one another, to build solidarity, and to search for peace. Our participatory research with people who know firsthand what it means to be victimized by stereotypes led us to a new understanding of the violence of poverty, of what it means to break the silence about this violence, and of the choices people make to work toward peace.

- **Governance for peace rooted in the struggle to overcome poverty.** This chapter addresses how ATD Fourth World structures its internal governance in a way that promotes effective and inclusive projects. This governance ensures that people living in poverty are fully involved in all aspects of decision making and that our work remains rooted in their experiences, ideas, and aspirations. The chapter also shares some insights that we think should also be applied to public decision making with respect to co-responsibility, intercultural intelligence, and an ethical approach to confrontation.

- **Courage amid conflict in the Central African Republic.** During the conflict that started in 2013, our members took great risks to continue organizing Street Libraries with children and to support their most vulnerable neighbors. In this landlocked country with limited communications infrastructure, people's thirst for training and for learning about the world is striking. Since the 1980s, over decades of instability, we have had a Volunteer Corps team there bearing witness to the strength and creativity of Central Africans.

Acknowledgments

Principal contributor

Eugen Brand

Additional contributors

Marina Mingot Acuña, Rosana Santa Ana, Laudan Aron-Turnham, Françoise Barbier, Lydia Bayo, Gérard Bureau, Catherine Calaguas, Brendan Coyne, Typhaine Cornacchiari, Caroline Cugnet, Bruno Dabout, Véronique Davienne, Lucien Duquesne, Elda Flandrois, Yaque Guzman-Oviedo, Philippe Hamel, Rosemarie Hoffmann-Tran, Jérémy Ianni, Charlene Igano, Alvaro Iniesta, Josephine Javier, Vanessa Joos, Susan Lanzuela, Cristina Lim-Yuson, Jhiwsel Luna-Rios, Bert Luyts, Guy Malfait, Huguette Redegeld-Bossot, Ton Redegeld, Pierre Saglio, Jean-Christophe Sarrot, Bruno Tardieu, Lilian Tiglao, Jean Tonglet, and Thierry Viard

Support and editing

Moya Amateau, Rosa J. Cho, Jill Cunningham, Romain Fossey, Claude Heyberger, Patricia Heyberger, Rosemarie Hoffmann-Tran, Jane R. Hsiao, Colette Jay, Catherine Lopes, Kristy McCaskill, Anne Monnet, Elizabeth Naumann, Janet Nelson, Béatrice Noyer, Marylise Roy, and Alain Souchard

Cover, interior design, and composition

Leigh McLellan Design

Printed in Great Britain
by Amazon